BOATSY
Inside the Forest
Executive Crew

Gary Clarke and Martin King

Headhunter Books

First published in September 2005 by Head-Hunter Books
This paperback editon 2006

Copyright © 2005 Martin King and Gary Clarke

ISBN 0 9548542 7 6

Head-Hunter Books

Photographs by:
Martin King, Louisa Mansfield, Gary D Marriott and Gary Lee Clarke.

Printed in Great Britain by Creative Print and Design

BOATSY
Inside the Forest
Executive Crew

LADIES AND GENTLEMEN

Welcome To a meeting of the Forest Executive Crew. Please remain seated throughout the proceedings for your own safety. Those of a nervous disposition should turn back now and under no circumstances look through these pages.

YOU HAVE BEEN WARNED.

Foreword

When I was about 10, me and lots of the other kids that lived in my area would play football out in the street. The goal posts would be two jumpers or coats thrown down, sometimes up to 10 yards apart, and the length of the pitch could be anything from 20ft to 200 yards long. One of the kids who would play out regularly would often come out with a big hand-knitted, red and white scarf tied around his neck. Pinned on it was a little, red plastic, star-shaped badge, which had a black and white photo in the middle of it. I was curious and asked him who the bloke was in the photo.

"That's Joe Baker," said the kid.

"Joe who?" I asked.

"Joe Baker, he plays centre forward for Nottingham Forest," he replied.

"Why have you got his picture pinned on an Arsenal or Man Utd scarf?" I asked him.

The kid laughed and touched his scarf. "These are the colours of Nottm. Forest," he said proudly.

That happened around 1966 and he was the first Forest fan I'd ever met. A couple of years later Chelsea were playing Forest at Stamford Bridge and me and a couple of mates came off the tube at Fulham Broadway and were walking towards the ground. We stopped and bought a programme each and then got ourselves a hot-dog from one of them mobile burger stalls. We carried on walking towards the Shed End entrance when we were surrounded by as gang of longhaired greasers in leather jackets with red and white scarves tied around their necks. One of them grabbed my Chelsea scarf, which was hanging loosely around my neck, and walked away laughing.

"Oi," I shouted, "bring that back," and I chased after him. All his mates were laughing as he dangled my scarf in front of me.

"Does the little kiddie want his scarf back?" he mocked. I was close to tears. Me Nan had knitted that scarf for me and she'd taken ages to complete it. My mates stood around looking but we were hopeless, we couldn't do nothing, here we were, about 12 years of age, and these Forest boys were in their late teens and some even well into their twenties. One of them had seen enough and was more than likely their leader.

"Right, you've had your fun, give the kid his scarf back," he said. The red-faced youth dropped the scarf into my waiting hands and turned and walked away. I laughed out loud. That Forest kid had made himself look a right mug.

Inside the ground the Shed end quickly began to fill up as we stood right at the back under the cover. We couldn't see a thing but we didn't care. We were only in there for the atmosphere and to tell our friends at school on the Monday morning that we'd watched the game against Forest from the back of the Shed where all the top lads stood. Just before kick off we found ourselves being pushed forward from behind. "Forest, Forest, Forest," echoed around under the tin roof of the Shed. A no-man's gap appeared between us and the Forest fans that had infiltrated the Shed. They'd come along the narrow walkway at the back and then ducked under the metal barriers and surged in behind where we'd been standing, and by the looks of it they were the same bunch that had tried to pinch my scarf. The Old Bill quickly surrounded them and took them down the terraces and off to the right and under the old East Stand and put them with the rest of the Forest fans under the old North Stand, which was the peculiar looking stand that looked like it was on stilts.

A few years after these events I was travelling up to Leicester to watch Chelsea and I happened to be in the same carriage as the Chelsea hierarchy, Eccles and Greenaway, who were holding court. Greenaway, who was a terrace legend and leader of The Shed, was a good 15 years older than us lads so we were in truly great company and hung on his every word. He told us of his adventures following his beloved Chelsea and how he and a few other lads had originally got The Shed boys organized. I remember him saying how he and a few of the lads had gone up to Nottingham for a game, and on arriving they left the station in dribs and drabs and set off for the ground. In them days there was no such thing as police escorts as it was every man for himself. They came under attack from a mob of Forest fans who Mick said were highly organised. A few Chelsea lads suffered cuts and bruises and vowed after that game to be as organised as the Forest firm they'd encountered.

At the game at Leicester we infiltrated the home fans' end and ran them into an enclosure along the side. They re-grouped and sang at us Chelsea fans, standing in their end, "You'll never take the Forest. You'll never take the Forest." How embarrassing for them having to sing about their far tougher neighbours. It reminded me of a little kid fighting another kid and saying, "I'll get my big brother on you, you wouldn't be able to beat him up. He's tougher than you."

The first time I went to the City ground was during the 75/76 season when we won 3-1. It was a bitterly cold, grey January day up there in a Division Two game. Goals from Ray Wilkins, Ian Hutchinson and Bill Garner won it for us but it was off the pitch where the real action happened. British Rail ran a football special up there from London and we arrived about 1.30. We gave a chant of "Chelsea, Chelsea," which echoed around the high roof of the station. We pushed past the ticket inspectors on the barriers and chased a few Forest fans off that had come to take a look at our arrival. We came out into the street and were met by the police and half a dozen police horses. By sheer weight of numbers we swept past them and turned left out of the station and headed towards Trent Bridge and the ground. On our right were a couple of pubs and some Forest came out to have a go. By now the Old Bill had caught up with us and got in between them and us. A few bottles were thrown and we headed off over the bridge. Half way across, a mob of Forest came towards us from the right and we slipped out of the police escort and walked towards them. There was about 30 of us and the same number of them.

"Come on Forest, we're Chelsea," we said, and they backed off. We had them walking backwards all the way over the bridge and as we reached the other side a 200-strong Forest mob appeared. Chelsea burst through the Old Bill and scattered Forest everywhere. Now we were on our own. A programme seller was robbed as we cleared the queuing Forest fans outside the Trent end turnstiles. We walked around the ground towards the East Stand and standing behind a wire fence was another mob of Forest who, because of the fence, thought they were safe. A few Chelsea scrambled over the top of the fence and dropped in amongst the Forest and blows were exchanged. The rest of the Chelsea set about ripping the fence down and within minutes it was toe-to-toe. Another programme seller was robbed of his money and programmes, as we were pushed towards the turnstiles by the police. Once inside it soon became clear that the Forest mob we'd been fighting with outside, were standing in another section of terracing next to us. When Chelsea scored, the fighting started and it carried on for a few minutes before the Old Bill restored order.

In the second half, most of the Forest mob went and stood behind the goal on the West Bridgeford end. A couple of hundred of us managed to get past the Old Bill and got up there and clashed with them. It was fucking mental and I'll give it to Forest, they were as game as fuck and gave as good as they got. We had a top firm in the mid 70s and I'd put Forest on a par with us. After the game, it was dark and as we got outside Forest launched attack after attack on us. On the bridge there was a right old battle as police on horseback cleared a path for us back to the station.

The following season we played them in the November up at Nottingham. This time we had two football specials up there and the Old Bill had their act together and there was no real trouble outside before the game. We were given the Trent end, which at the time we thought we'd gone in there and taken it, and saw that as a result. We had seven thousand fans up there that day. A couple of hundred of our finest had slipped the Old Bill outside and went into the bottom of the East Stand on the corner of the West Bridgeford terraces. It went mental in there with Forest coming at our boys from all angles in the end our boys were taken out by the Old Bill and marched around the pitch and put in the Trent End with us. Outside there was running battles and lots of us, wary of the tales of Forest catching visiting fans and throwing them off of the Trent Bridge and into the river, stuck together like glue. We done well all the way over the bridge until we reached the other side when it got a bit messy, we were being stretched as bottles and bricks rained down on us. It wasn't looking good; you had to have your wits about you as Forest came into us from all directions, every street corner we came to would mean another Forest attack. In the end we made it back to the station but it was well on top all the way from the ground. A few of ours were nicked and a few were injured but on the train journey back to London, we all commented on just how game the Forest lads were. At that game, there was something like nine stabbings, which at the time I think was a record at an English football match.

Over the years Forest have always had a top firm and I've had the utmost respect for them. One thing's sure, they're no mugs, and anyone who says they are don't have a clue what they're talking about.

Martin King.
September '05

Acknowledgements

Gary would like to thank all the top Forest boys who have sadly passed away over the years.
Gez Mullen, Paul Scarrett, Mark Anderson, Alfie, Jim Molineux, Wadon and Killer from Sutton. – All missed, R.I.P.

My Grandma. All the Forest firm over the years for making it a roller coaster ride, i.e. One Punch, our main boy, Dale C, Kirky, Scriv, Ginger, Shaun, my best mate, Skeeny, Pele, Lindo, Parma, Tim, Butler, Ryan and Lenny. Claire, my first girl-friend and life long mate. Nat for putting up with the hooligan next door, and Arthur Meash.

The Newcastle boys, Peet my best mate up North, Jonny Sharpe, Eddie, Tes, Joey, Daz B, and John from Sheffield for introducing me to the Geordie boys. Graham and Whitey from north of the border, Deacon, Piper H from Wales. All the lads in Thailand for making our annual hols a top time. Chubby Chris, Jeff, Steve, Spence from Oldham and Gary from Man U. All top boys. Ashley from Prague, Phil in Amsterdam and my mates in Cologne. Mark, Daz and Bern at work. Martin King for writing and putting up with my drunkenness at his house, and his family. Cass Pennant. H.M.P. Wealstun for teaching me to use the computer. My half American sister, mum and dad for finally giving up on me at 40 ha!ha! and all the 55 that turned up in Benidorm for my recent 40th bash. The Forest young boys, Adam, Fred and Glynn. Thanks to Louisa M for taking the photos in Chichester and for looking so beautiful, Thanks to Bill Middleton at The Hornet Tattoo Studio in Chichester for The Forest tattoo "Cheers Bill you did a brilliant job and a top man"

Cheers boys it's been a laugh.

Contents

Contents

CHAPTER 1

From Little Acorns Grow?

MY FULL name is Gary Lee Clarke and I was born in 1965 in Sneinton, Nottingham. My parents told me that I sat up in my cot when I was aged one and watched the 1966 World Cup final between England and West Germany.

My dad is a Cambridge United fan who originates from Cambridge, and my mum is a local girl from Nottingham. They met on a night out when dad came up with a few of his mates. I was their first mistake and five years later my sister Julie arrived!

Growing up in Sneinton was great fun. The streets were like what you see on Coronation Street. The houses had no front gardens and had small back yards. All the kids would play out in the streets, either riding up and down on their bikes or playing football in the middle of the road.

My first school was Bluebell Hill and then I went to primary school up near the old public baths, and they were great times. I loved school and loved the company of all the other kids. While at Bluebell Hill I made my first television appearance. I was about five years old and was filmed walking into school and running around the playground like a mad kid, along with all the other kids showing off for the cameras. It was shown on T.V. in black and white in a documentary type programme.

Just after my sister was born the family moved to Silverdale. It's just near Clifton, which is seen as a posh part of Nottingham. We'd moved to a bigger house, which was a very modern 70s style semi-detached property. My dad was a long distance lorry driver and I remember as a young boy he'd take me up to places like Glasgow and deliver to the markets up there. I'd sit next to him and imagine it was me driving the truck. My mum worked at 'Pork Farms', which was well known in Nottingham for making sausages and pork pies. She worked on the production line.

When I started my junior school at Brooksby I got into the school football team, I'd say I was better than average player. At the school most of the kids supported Forest and during the winter they would either have a red and white knitted Forest scarf tied around their necks or one of the red and white silk, shiny scarves tied around their wrist. A lot of the boys would also have a second favourite team with loads following Liverpool or Man United. Mine was Leeds United, I loved the look of the kit and the white blue and yellow scarf stood out it just looked so different.

Around this time I managed to nag my dad into taking me to see Forest at the City ground. Dad coming from Cambridge had a soft spot for the East Anglian sides and agreed to take me to see Forest at home to Norwich City. It was the 74/75 season and Forest had just sold the terrace idol, Duncan McKenzie, for £240,000 to Leeds United. For me it didn't bother me I didn't mind that, what with Leeds being my second team, but a lot of Forest fans were up in arms about his transfer and saw no way of ever getting out of the Second Division and back with the big boys and back to First Division football.

Just dad and me travelled down to the ground by bus, and as we got off he stopped and bought me a big, red and white Forest rosette and pinned it on my chest. I was over the moon and was the proudest lad in the whole of Nottingham. As we walked towards the ground with thousands of other people, I'd glance down every couple of seconds and fiddle with this huge rosette. My grin went from ear to ear and I was loving it. The Forest captain Sammy Chapman, got sent off that day and most of the thirteen thousand crowd went home unhappy as we slumped to a 3-1 defeat. We were fourth from bottom and manager, Alan Brown, only lasted another few months before being replaced by fans' choice for the job, Brian Clough. Funny thing was, Duncan McKenzie was Cloughie's first big signing in his very short stay as Leeds United's manager. What would the pair had of achieve together at Forest? Who knows?

At the time I didn't realise that Forest had a hooligan firm but the name Scarrett would often crop up in the school playground.
    "Paul Scarrett done this on Saturday" or "Scarrett did this".
Paul Scarrett's name in Nottingham was as well known as Robin Hood. Every kid in my school claimed to be in his gang and tales of him were legendary. I never went to another Forest game until the following season but my granddad, who was a Notts County fan, would take me along to

watch County. It was 20p for me to get in but over at Forest it was that bit dearer at 25p. But then you have to pay that bit more for class.

In the promotion year of '76 I began to go and watch the team on a regular basis. There was trouble at nearly every home game. For a young, impressionable lad it was a real eye-opener. I also watched a lot of football on the telly and if there was a big, live game on the radio I'd tune in and listen with the radio and my head under the covers so as not to disturb mum and dad. They had sent me off to bed hours before and were expecting me to be fast asleep. I was a regular listener to Radio 2 and around this time, Leeds was playing in European cups, and most of their games were broadcast.

In the fashion stakes green, nylon flight jackets were in vogue which were the jackets worn by The Mad Squad, of which Scarrett was the leader. Me grandma, me mum's mum, would often treat me and she funded my shopping trips. I remember her giving me the money to go out and buy a flight jacket and a pair of baggy trousers with side pockets, and a pair of Dr. Martens.

I loved my football and played for Clifton Rangers, a local boys' side. I was only 11 when the team went out to Sweden to play in a European youth tournament. We got through to the quarterfinals but went out on penalties. Lots of the boys from that side went on to play semi-pro football and even Viv Anderson of Forest, Arsenal, Man United and England fame, once played for Clifton.

When I was about 13 my dad's mate got sent to prison for fighting in a local pub so I was given his season ticket because he knew I was a big Forest fan, and he knew I'd use it. That was in 1977, the year we won the League and were crowned champions. I witnessed some great football and some even better rows on the terraces. On the field of play, it was some achievement that what some people would call a small club, could win the League title, but we had some truly great players in that side. Well, to me, all eleven were great players, and each and every one of them performed to their highest level. Week in and week out they worked their socks off to get the results, which earned us the title. Plus we had the great man in charge. The last game of the season saw us draw 0-0 with Liverpool up at Anfield, and they finished second in the League, seven points behind us. We also beat them after a re-play to win the League Cup that season.

Off the pitch battles raged on the terraces with Chelsea at home, before during and after the game, with Liverpool at home and away in the league, and in the cup games, and against Leeds in the two legged League Cup semi-finals. However, all these rows I watched from the safety of an expensive seat, courtesy of me dad's mate! It was the same when we played Derby in what I think was Brian Clough's testimonial game at the City ground. Derby bought thousands over and it was the first time I felt the pure hatred between the two sets of fans. Well, it certainly opened my eyes as to how much the two sets of fans hated one another.

I got myself a morning paper round for the local corner shop and all went well for a few months. I even copied the other lads who, before loading the newspapers into their delivery bags, would line the bottom of the bag with Mars Bars, Twix's, Crunchies and all sorts of sweets and bars of chocolate. I'd stroll the streets on my round with a gob full of chocolate and read the back pages on what the news was in the world of football. It was a cushy little number until the shop owner got wind of what was going on and checked everyone's paper sacks before they were allowed to leave the shop. But it got even worse when the police turned up at my house and asked mum and dad if they could have a word with them about parcels going missing from people's doorsteps. When I was out on my paper round, I'd often see the postman leaving parcels on people's doorsteps. He'd ring the front doorbell or rattle the letterbox, and if there were no answer, he'd leave the parcel on the doorstep. My curiosity got the better of me and being a nosey kid I'd pick the parcel up, pop it into my sack, walk around the corner and open it up. Most of it was catalogue stuff like perfume or shoes, or cheap jewellery. I'd usually sling it over the hedge into someone's front garden or dump it down a side alleyway. Anyway, it turned out that my mate, who had a round in another part of town, had been caught doing the same as me and to try and save his own skin had grassed me up and said that I'd put the idea into his head. Dad was having none of it and told the coppers to piss off.

The secondary school I'd not long started at was, at one time, an all-girls school and had only been running as a mixed school for about a year. The majority of the pupils were girls, but it wasn't long before I found myself in the school football team. I was a good utility player in the mould of Leeds United's Paul Madley. I played in goal, centre-half, winger, and centre forward. I'm not being bigheaded but I was good and comfortable in any position, but my favourite position was in mid-field and from that position I scored quite a few goals. A rumour went around the school that Forest had, on more than one occasion, sent down an undercover scout to watch a few of the lads, but more likely if they were watching they'd have been looking at my best mate and our best player Stuart Hopps, he was the star of our side. Before every game, I'd scan the vast crowd. Well half a dozen people might be watching if we were lucky and I'd make a mental note of who just might just be the scout. If he were undercover then he'd have the collar of his sheepskin coat pulled up, sunglasses on and his trilby hat pulled down so that the brim was resting on the tip of his nose! Perhaps I watched to much telly as a kid?

We were playing a game against St. Bernadette's at their school field and my grandparents came up from Cambridge to watch me. They were as proud as punch to see their grandson turning out for his school. I felt good in my amber and black striped shirt as the ref checked with his linesman, held the whistle to his mouth and blew to get the proceedings
Underway, all went well, and I was seeing a lot of the ball and was probing and prodding and making some good runs and passes. I went into a tackle on the line with one of their players and it came off of him for a throw in to us.

"It's our ball," said the kid.

"How do you work that out?" I replied.

With that he spat at me and I just went mad and went for him and was shouting and cursing and calling him all the cunts and mother-fuckers in the world. The thing is the ref. and the linesman only heard me swearing and didn't see the kid spit at me, so I was sent off for abusive language. My mum and dad and grandparents from Cambridge were horrified and I didn't know where to put my face as I trudged off dejected. Also watching was my mum's dad from Nottingham, and for months afterwards he refused to speak to me.

The next day I was called into the headmaster's office and he was not a happy man. He laid down the law to me and told me, in no uncertain terms that I'd brought shame upon myself and the school. I had to send a letter of apology to the headmaster at St. Bernadette's and was banned for two games. Just before the end of the season, after I'd served my ban I was sent off yet again for fighting with one of my own players. We had a right greedy cunt in our team called Simon James who just got the ball and hogged it and refused to pass to anyone else. I called him a greedy wanker, and went for him and hit him. My teacher was the referee and sent me off and that was me finished in the football team. Just before I left school for good, I wasn't even allowed to play in the end of term teachers versus pupils match. I was gutted.

The 78-79 season saw Forest win the European Cup against Malmo of Sweden in front of 80,000 fans in the Olympic Stadium, Munich. A Trevor Francis header just before half- time won the famous trophy for us. Trevor had once been Britain's most expensive footballer when Brian Clough paid Birmingham City a million pound minus one penny for his services. I watched the game on telly at home with my dad, and him and me were jumping for joy as the captain, John McGovern, lifted the huge cup above his head.

The following year we were back in the final to defend our crown against Kevin Keegan's club, Hamburg, in Madrid. From the opening kick-off we had to defend as we were pinned back by wave after wave of German attacks. I think we only managed one shot on goal in the first twenty minutes but soon after that we scored when winger, John Robertson, played a one-two with centre forward Gary Birtles, staggered forward another couple of paces, and unleashed a shot which curled around the diving keeper and nestled in the bottom corner of the net. The Forest fans in the stadium erupted in a sea of red and white and deafening noise, a bit like our front room as dad and me did a victory jig together! Somehow, we held on, with some stirling defensive work and some world class saves from keeper Peter Shilton. When the ref. blew for full time I jumped from my chair and punched the air with clenched fists. Mum got up seemingly not that impressed by it all.

"Would anyone like a cup of tea?" she asked.

Just before the end of the football season my mum and dad had taken me and me sister down to visit our grandparents in Cambridge. Dad suggested we go and watch Cambridge United play Chelsea so off we went we paid to get in and made our way up the terraces, and stopped at a place on the crumbling concrete steps, as the ground began to fill up. The tiny open space at the far end was where the majority of Chelsea fans were packed in. Suddenly the crowds around us began to push backwards and a huge gap in the crowd appeared as a group of Chelsea fans had come onto the home team's terracing. Words were exchanged between the two sets of fans as they flew into one another with fists and boots. A copper on his own dived in to separate them and lashed out with his fists, but as he drew his hand back to throw a punch, he cracked me straight on the nose. Fucking hell, did it hurt? I had tears in my eyes as dad quickly moved me away from the trouble. I was shocked. All I remember was that it was all over the Sunday papers the next day as Chelsea fans went on the rampage around Cambridge after the game.

It wasn't long after that that the cricket season started. I was a keen cricketer and played for the school cricket team as the opening bat. I also played a good standard of cricket for Notts Forest Cricket Club where, at the age of 13, I won the Young Player of the Year award and for some reason or other. I never went to collect it. One day I bunked off of school and went to watch a Test match, it was either against the West Indies or Australia, anyway, my

English teacher spots me there and reports back to the headmaster. I'm called to his office and given a letter to take home to my parents and given detention. I signed it myself forging dad's signature, do the detention and mum and dad are none the wiser. See, all those years of reading The Bash Street Kids and Winker Watson did pay off and I did learn something!

At 15 I played for local cricket side, Melbourne, who were a top men's side. I played with them up until I was 17 and only stopped playing for them when two coppers joined the club and started asking questions about my background. I owned a season ticket to watch Notts county cricket team for a good few years, and I still enjoy me cricket and go to quite a few Test matches.

NAME: Meash
AGE: 52
CLUB: Nottingham Forest

I first went in '67 and it was a friendly against the shit and I can't even bring myself to say their name. There wasn't a lot of trouble. It was no big deal. I was about 14 and went with a few mates that lived on The Meadows estate. Joe Baker was playing for Forest in them days and he was a legend on the field and off it. We also had the legends on the terraces. From 68/69 I think football hooliganism was in full swing. I went through the whole lot, skinheads, suedeheads, and the whole bag of bollocks. I read all the Richard Allen books, wore all the gear. One thing I never done was have a drink at football. I'd go in the boozer with all the lads but I'd have a lemonade as I wanted to keep my wits about me if it went off. I was a serious player and I wasn't bothered about the football. I didn't want to get nicked so alcohol could never get in the way. I thought of myself as a serious player, a front line lad. People had respect for me, they knew I was game and I didn't realise it until years later when a few lads pointed out to me just how well respected I'd been at Forest. I didn't do it for that fact. I didn't want to be the top boy or a hard man. I done it for my team and it was something I wanted to do. It was as simple as that. I'm not ashamed of anything I done in them days. The young boys now have it all stacked against them. They can't recreate what we did or what we had. If they do something now it can come back to haunt them 6 months later, where if we had a row and didn't get nicked there and then you were safe and you'd got away with it. Nowadays it's so different. Nowadays there's no such thing as taking another team's end. You're allocated a ticket and that's where you have to sit. The fun has been taken out of it. It was just boys acting like boys, nothing too serious. A fight in some other team's end was the highlight of the day. If you got a good hiding or not and if your team won or lost, you loved it. I'd heard of Boatsy long before I met him and if he was around in my time the bloke would be a legend. Dale and Ronnie are the same types, decent lads who are as game as fuck and would have been the top boys in the very early days. I've got nothing but respect for them all, but if I hadn't ducked out of the football scene a few years back then I'm sure I would now be sitting in a prison cell doing a long sentence.

Above: Me and gran on the street where I was born.

Top right: Throwing a moody (starting early), family holiday at Maplethorpe.

Below: 'Robin hood', Sherwood Forest.

Botton right: Me with sister when she was born (two gremlins).

CHAPTER 2

Spuds, Carrots, Apples, and Two Black Eyes

I LEFT SCHOOL at 15 with seven C.S.E.s and was advised by mum and dad to try to get a decent job or get an apprenticeship. As I was leaving school, my sister was just starting but to tell you the truth, as kids we didn't really have a lot to do with one another. I started a Y.T.S. Scheme for the local council doing building work and repairs, in Nottingham. The best jobs going though, were working for Players Cigarettes or Boots the Chemist in their warehouse, and if you were from the outskirts of Nottingham, you might get a job in the mines.

I was hanging around with Ashley White at the local youth club. He was a few years older than me and he wore all the latest gear, followed Forest everywhere and always had money in his pocket. I looked up to him and wanted to be just like him. I had the wedge haircut done by "Top Notch" hairdressers in Nottingham. I dressed like I was a member of The Human League or Duran Duran.

One Saturday a few mates and me decided to go and watch Notts County at home to Leeds. At the time, Leeds had a decent following around Nottingham and tales of their Service Crew were legendary. I was sixteen and wasn't really into women or puffing dope. I was just into me clothes, having a good drink and watching football. After the game, there were Leeds' fans everywhere. At the time Notts County could muster a firm of say, 30 or 40, but against someone like Leeds they knew they'd be out-numbered so they wouldn't bother turning out. I was just walking and talking with me mates, when a bloke came bowling through the crowds, arms pumping up and down by his side as if he was on some kind of mission. He came crashing into me and nearly knocked me flying. I've stopped and give it the biggen.

"Watch ya self mate" I said, and with that a copper grabs me and leads me off and throws me in the back of a police van and drives off to Shire Hall police station. It's the place where they used to hang people and is now a museum. Because I was so big I looked older than I was and when the copper interviewed me and found out how old I was, he said if he had known my age he wouldn't have arrested me. After a couple of hours in the cell's my dad was called and he came up to collect me in his car. He looked unhappy but didn't stay cross for to long. I think he had the hump more with the coppers than with me but I knew he'd calmed down when he dropped me off outside the local pub. I'd been shitting myself in the police station as they banged me up in a cell, which was once a dungeon, so I was in need of a pint.

I lasted in the job with the council for six months but really wanted to find another job that paid more than the £23 a week I was getting. My next job was down at the fruit and veg market where I'd heard that one of the traders was looking for a barrow boy, we had a brief chat, and I was fixed up with the job. It was a family run business and I was on a little bit more money but with tips, some weeks I was going home with over £30, plus I was eating healthily with all them apples, bananas, pears, and grapes ready waiting there to be eaten for nothing. The one drawback was that I had to get up at 3.45 a.m. to catch the postmen and milkmen's bus. It was six days a week but most days I was done by 8.00 a.m. It was a mad rush for four hours with me rushing about like a blue arsed fly, loading up vans and trucks. However, the plus side was that the market pub opened at 5.30 a.m. so as soon as we finished work I'd have a couple of pints and then head off home. Even at that time of the morning the pub was buzzing and was jam-packed.

On a Saturday it was great. I'd finish and go straight in the pub and stand around talking with me workmates about that day's game. There was loads of Forest fans that worked there and the banter and piss taking was excellent. Also on a Saturday if I was off to the game, I'd get picked up by me mates, straight from work.

It was around this time that I first met the legendary Paul Scarrett in the flesh, and I wasn't disappointed. He was a lovely fella but a complete nutcase. He was fearless. If there was a pub full of fans from another team he'd think nothing of steaming into them on his own. I was once in court for coming out of a nightclub pissed up, and was arrested for criminal damage. It was my very first court appearance for which I received a fine. On the same day Scarrett was also in court for something or other but was held on remand. When he came out we would regularly meet up and bump into one another in the pubs around Nottingham. He could actually handle himself and worked the doors of the pubs and clubs around Skegness, but trouble never seemed to be far from him. He did all sorts of work to earn a few bob to follow Forest and England, and at one time was doing a bit of building work.

Forest had by now won two European Cups and the future looked bright, but the club couldn't keep the momentum going and finished a disappointing 7th in the 1980/81 season.

The following season I was again in bother and found myself making another court appearance. I got a lift up to Blackburn to watch Forest and somehow or another found myself in the home end next to the Forest fans, in the away fans section. I was talking to a couple of mates I knew through the metal fence, which kept the fans apart. A copper comes across to me, grabs me and throws me out of the ground because he said I was having a go at the visiting fans. I gave him a bit of lip back and told him to get a life, as I was a Forest fan. With that he throws me into the back of the police van and starts kicking and punching me. He was a big, strong fucker, probably in his early twenties, but he gave me a bit of a kicking. I didn't know whether to hit him back or not and was a bit confused and I decided against it because it would have just made matters worse. Once he'd booked me in at the police station, I never saw him again. I was charged and released after a few hours. I went to court a few weeks later where I pleaded "not guilty" to the charges. I also put in a counter complaint about the police, but the copper who bashed me wasn't in court. Eventually it went to trial and I had witnesses to the incident. Again, this copper failed to show so the judge threw the case out and I never heard another thing.

Now I was going further afield to buy the latest fashions. I'd go to Sharp Sports in Kensington High Street to buy the Fila, Lacoste and Tacchini gear. I'd also travel up to the Arndale Centre in Manchester to buy faded jeans. We had two good sports shops in Nottingham but they didn't have the choice that the shops in London had. When Pringle hit the streets of Nottingham, Jessops, one of the leading men's shops in the city, would get robbed left, right and centre. The trick was to take two Pringle diamond jumpers into the changing rooms with you, slip one on and put a coat or jumper over the top of it, come out the changing rooms and hang one back up on the rails. It worked a treat and at one time, everyone was pulling that stroke. We'd also nick golf jackets and Slazenger gear the same way. My last resort if I had no other choice, was to get my grandma May to pay for it. She used to spoil me rotten and would buy me anything. She was a smashing lady and I had a special relationship with her; there was a real bond between us. She was born on the 1st of May, hence her name.

With the football I'm now going home and away to nearly every game. One game we had Arsenal away but I didn't go. About 30 of our young lot got attacked by a mob of Arsenal outside a pub near the ground. A good mate of mine had a bottle smashed in his face and he ended up having over 20 stitches. The following year we were out for revenge and we got a mob up of sorts. Most of our main faces were in prison for a fight up in Middlesborough a few years earlier. So 53 of us young lot, set off from Nottingham to Highbury. For this particular game up at Boro we took a couple of battle buses up there which are basically coaches which are full of lads who don't mind a row, hence the name 'battle bus' After the game there was running battles on the streets. We had Boro on the back foot, one of their lads who stood was punched, and he hit his head on the stone kerb, as he went down. It turned out he only had a thin skull and he sadly died from his injuries. Because of this incident, many of our main characters were banged up.

When we got down to London we met up with a few more of our lot and made our way by tube, over to Arsenal. We had a couple of the older lads at the front leading us who seemed to know what they were doing so we let them get on with it and happily tagged on behind. Outside the stadium, we never saw any Arsenal lads so we entered the ground at the Clock End. It was a funny set up at Highbury in them days because you had to walk through the Arsenal fans to get to the "away" fans' section and all that separated you was a line of plastic ticker tape. I stood out like a sore thumb with my wedge haircut, faded jeans and a Pringle jumper. It was obvious I was a Northerner by the way I was dressed. By the time I'd crossed into our section I was covered from head to toe in spit; it was disgusting, and the Old Bill just stood around and laughed. We only had about 200 fans there in total because at the time our away support was shite.

After the game we got straight on the tube and told some Gooners, who were hanging around outside, to come back to Kings Cross if they fancied it. When we got back there they had a 100 strong mob waiting for us and it went mental, with running battles in the streets around the station. We gave as good as we got and never bottled in once. The traffic came to a standstill as we chased the main bulk of them up a side street. A copper, with another on a horse, shouted for us to stop, and more coppers appeared either end of the street and blocked us in. No one could get away.

"Right, you're all under arrest," said the copper on the horse.

"What for?" a few of us asked.

They nicked 30 of us all in one hit and charged us all with threatening behaviour at Holborn police station. A copper at the police station told me that I was to appear at Clerkenwell Magistrates Court on this certain date. When I told him I couldn't make that date he shook his head and looked at me in a strange, disbelieving way and then I explained to him that I was due in court in Leicester on the same date. What had happened was about 80 of us had gone into Leicester on a stag do and a fight had started. We very rarely played one another in those days because we were in different divisions, but we'd often go into Leicester for a night out on the piss. I was arrested for threatening behaviour and in court I received a £250 fine. The next day I was back down in London for that court appearance and pleaded not guilty, as had all the other lads on their appearance the day before. I had to go to London by train on my own, but we were all booked in together for a two-day trial at Lambeth Magistrates Court. We were all found guilty on the evidence of the two coppers that had originally stopped us. It was a set up, a kangaroo court, and a complete farce. There was only going to be one outcome, one verdict, and that, as I say, was guilty. I was one of the youngest and got an £80 fine and a couple of our main lads got £120 and £140 fines. But it was worth getting nicked for the night out we had out on the piss around the Elephant and Castle, while we were attending the court. How mum and dad felt about me getting into trouble at football had completely gone out of the window, but it didn't bother grandma. She came on the train with me to the court at Leicester and even paid my fine, bless her.

I think drink played a big part in my life at the time and away from football I was often being arrested for stupid things when I was pissed up, like threatening behaviour or criminal damage, really silly, daft things. My boss at the market though was a diamond geezer and although he laughed at my exploits, would still stick by me. I would turn up nearly every Monday morning for work with black eyes. I was a tall, well-built kid, and I wouldn't say I was particularly good at fighting but I was as game as fuck. I'd steam straight into anybody. I didn't care.

The young lot I was in with were getting a right reputation. We'd taken over from our older lot who were still inside for the Boro fight, and a few more got prison sentences for a fight in town when a Geordie had his ear ripped off with a metal roadside lantern. A few of the lads from the Middlesborough fight ended up doing their sentences in Durham prison, hence the friendship between us and the Newcastle lads. Well, nearly all Geordies liked us except the one that had his ear chopped off! The boys inside said the Geordie boys really looked after them and were fantastic, and they have the greatest respect for them, and just like the Geordies, our lot hated the Mackems and their sneaky ways. Everywhere we went now, there was trouble. We had no Old Bill on our case following us about and had total freedom to cause havoc. At our home games, we'd find a pub near to the railway station and by eleven o'clock we'd have a good mob together. Any visiting fans that came looking for it we'd find and sort them out. We never picked on scarfers or shirts and only fought with like-minded people. We were never bullies. It was like being a kid in a candy store and our little mob loved it.

One Saturday we had West Brom away and 30 of us went down by train to Birmingham New Street. From there, we caught a bus to the ground, got off and went straight into their end. They surrounded us with a big circle and it just went mental. It was toe-to-toe scrapping before the coppers moved in and separated us and took us down to the Forest end. Five minutes later a copper comes through the crowds, puts his hand on my shoulder, and tells me I'm under arrest for fighting in the home end. I can't believe it. All those people had been fighting and yet he picks me out. I'm charged and let out a few hours after the game. On the train on the way back North, there was a couple of carriages full of Geordies who were on their way home to Newcastle after playing at nearby Coventry City. Nearly all of them had something Burberry on and a few of their younger ones wanted to fill me in. A few older lads stopped it and pointed out to them that they were bullies as I was on my own. As the train pulled in at Nottingham I stood up and told the whole carriage,

"This aint the last you've seen of me. I'm Forest and we've got you next week and we're coming in on the Metro from Sunderland to kick it off with you lot" With that I was off the train and up the platform at 100 mph with the open train door swinging on its hinges. The next day I'd arranged to meet my girlfriend Claire in town that evening we'd been seeing one another for a few months and things were getting quite serious between us. The thing was I was already on bail for another incident and part of the bail conditions were that I was not allowed within a mile of Nottingham city centre. So I had to be careful where we went and where we met. I was waiting for her outside our main football pub, The Tavern in the Town, when a copper strolls past me and sees me.

"Clarke, what are you doing here?" he said, pointing at me.

"Clarke, you're on a curfew aren't you?"

He gets on his radio and I can hear voices at the other end, the situation, don't look good. He puts his radio away and smiles.

"Right Clarke, you're under arrest".

The thing was he had me bang to rights and I couldn't run away because when he first came over to me he had slapped some handcuffs on and chained me to some metal railings. I was well fucked. A police van was called and I was whisked off to the central police station. My pockets were searched and emptied but in the back pocket of my jeans was the charge sheet from West Bromwich from the day before. They're straight on the phone to the West Midlands. "Yes" came the reply from the West Bromwich Old Bill, "he was one of the 16 Forest fans arrested for threatening behaviour after a mass brawl in the home end of the ground". I'm allowed one phone call and speak to Claire's mum and I asked her to pass on a message to Claire that I won't be able to meet her because I'd been arrested. She was most understanding. Claire's mum and dad had split up and she thought the world of me and treated me better than a son. She was a lovely woman. I'm held in custody until the Monday morning when I appear in court for breaking my bail condition. Sitting in court are Claire and my grandma and as I look at Claire I realise what a fool I'd been. She looked radiant, beautiful. She was a pretty little thing who was always immaculately turned out. I was remanded by the magistrates to Glen Parva Youth Offender's Centre. Claire bursts out crying as grandma sits there looking bewildered by it all. Mum and dad are away and I'm more worried about what they're going to say when they find out, plus I'm due in court at West Bromwich on the Thursday, so I need two lots of bail to get out. The wheels go in motion with my solicitor working his nuts off to get me out.

My first night inside I shared a cell with a burglar from Ilkeston. Most of the people in there thought they were it and were cocky, young twats, with most of them being burglars and petty thieves. Luckily, enough one of my mates is already in there. He'd been in there loads of times and knew the ropes. Gez Mullen was a fellow Forest fan, and took me under his wing we trained together most days down in the prison gym. He was an old hand and didn't give a fuck for anyone. In my defence, I got references from work and eventually got bail for the case down at West Brom, but in total still spent 12 days in jail. I got out on bail just before mum and dad, got home from holiday and good old grandma never ever grassed me up. Mum and dad only found out about me being inside after my sister told them about 12 years later.

Anderlect, away in the semi-finals of the UEFA Cup, was the next spot of bother I got into. We travelled over by ferry from Dover to Ostend on the Saturday before the game. On board was 40 of Man Utd's finest Cockney Reds and there was 8 of us but that didn't stop me from kicking it off. We were sitting drinking with a few of them in the bar area just after the ferry had set sail. One of them started slagging Forest off and that was it. I'd heard enough of his shit and nutted him straight in the face. The whole boat went up with glasses, tables, chairs flying backwards, and forwards through the air. In Bill Burford's book, "Amongst the Thugs", he writes that they turned the ferry around but that did'nt happen we were only 20 minutes from Ostend. When we docked, the Belgian riot police stormed on. I'd been kicked to fuck by these Cockney Reds and had been booted down a flight of stairs. All the optics behind the bar was smashed and with glass all over the floor, it looked like a bomb had gone off. I was covered in blood and a couple of blokes from Manchester and a couple of stewards off the boat helped to clean up my wounds. As I was leaving the toilet, having been tidied up, a bloke I'd not long been fighting with walked past.

"That's one of them", I shouted, and smacked him one. That was it. All hell broke out again. They nicked a load of Mancs and frog-marched them off the boat but as they were leaving, they pointed my mate, Kirk and me out to the Old Bill, so they nicked me, Kirk, and a little half-caste youth named Eddie, who was one of ours. We were chucked in the back of a police van and no sooner were the doors slammed shut than this little prick, Eddie, started mouthing off. I had me hands handcuffed behind my back but it didn't stop me from sticking the nut on him. When we got to the police station the Old Bill threw a Manc in with us. We were all still handcuffed but that didn't stop us using our feet and heads to knock the shit out of him. He squealed like a pig and screamed the place down. As soon as we heard the cell door opening we all quickly sat back down like nothing was happening. The Manc was lying on the floor writhing in agony, crying his eyes out. The coppers gave us all a couple of whacks around the head and pulled me up and dragged me out and threw me in a cell with clear, plastic panels so they could see what I was up to. Anyone would think I was Hannibal Lector. They throw more United fans in with my two Forest mates and all you could hear was these Mancs singing United songs. The adrenalin in me began to subside and with the vast quantities of booze I'd consumed I began to feel unwell. Next thing I'm throwing up and there's sick everywhere. The police just left me but came in the next morning and throw a mop and bucket at me and said, "clear up English pig", and made me clean the cell up. I was fucking steaming when they'd first brought me into the nick but I'd sobered up when they interviewed me that afternoon I just said I wasn't being funny but it wasn't my fault and that we never started it and that Man Utd had caused all the trouble and they were to blame. The copper agreed, saying that Man Utd fans were always in trouble and were bad boys, and with that he let us go. I couldn't believe it! We'd been let out without charge, and they even let all the Mancs go soon after. However, some of our boys had been robbed of their money and some of their gear had been taken from their hand luggage. The Mancs, while we had been fighting, had slashed our bags open and gone through them, the sort of trick the Scousers would pull. The United fans fucked off to Italy or wherever they were playing, and we stayed in Ostend another couple of nights.

The next night I was arrested again for climbing a flagpole and trying to nick a flag. I was taken to the same police station I'd just spent two days in.

As I walked in all the coppers recognised me and were laughing their bollocks off. They nicked me for drunk and disorderly, but released me without charge the next morning.

At the game it was brilliant. We went in their end about a hundred handed, and cleared it not once but three times. On the pitch we were 2-0 up from the first leg but lost 3-0 over there. We scored a perfectly good goal with a Paul Hart header but it was disallowed for no reason. They were also awarded a right dodgy penalty, which they scored from, it came out a few years back that the ref was bent and the game was proved to have been fixed. The ref died a few years ago and some players have received compensation for that game. I think, but I'm not 100 per cent sure, that the ref was Spanish, and if we had of got through we would have played Spurs in an all-English final.

The next season I was back in Belgium again for the first round of the UEFA Cup. We arrived Sunday afternoon, steaming drunk, and broke into a boat in the harbour and that's where we slept until the next morning. That's how drunk we were. We were up early looking for somewhere to get some breakfast when we've seen a postman out on his delivery, and when his back was turned, I whipped his sack from off the front of his bike and fucked off. All the boys with me were pissing themselves laughing and couldn't believe what I'd done. I went around the corner and opened up some of the parcels in the sack. I opened one up and inside were four large bundles of brand new unused Portuguese bank notes. I threw the sack away, and pocketed the money and during the course of the day went into various banks and exchanged the notes into Belgian francs and English money. Overall, there was £700 worth of these notes. I only left home with £30! I treated me mates to drinks and meals and a few of the lads went shop lifting in the Lacoste shop and came out with bundles of gear. The Belgians just didn't have a clue. I was now staying in a luxury hotel and the night before the game some of the hotel staff sussed out that a few of the lads were creeping into the hotel and were dossing down in my room. Once I was back in that night, they locked the front doors behind me and wouldn't let any of the other lads in. The only place they could kip was in the nearby shop doorways so I open my bedroom windows and throw out spare blankets and pillows so they could at least try to get some sleep in a bit of comfort. The hotel staff saw me doing this so they call the police who knock on my door, and arrest me and lock me up for two days. Thank God, I'd taken all the Lacoste gear out of their packets and taken the price tags off because when they searched my room they thought that all the nicked gear was just my normal clobber that I'd bought with me. The Belgian Old Bill aint the brightest in the world, I can tell you.

On the day of the game the cells in the police station were filling up rapidly until there was 50 Forest fans banged up. The following morning the Belgian police loaded us all into police vans and with sirens going and blue lights flashing they drove like lunatics through the streets. We stopped alongside a ferry in the Port of Zeebruger. We were then frog-marched up the gangway onto the waiting ferry and out of the country. No one was charged and they handed all our personal belongings back to us. The next day it was all over the British and Belgian papers. On my arrival back in England I headed straight to London and Sharps Sports in Kensington High Street and had a little bit of retail therapy with the money I had left over from my Belgian jolly!

I've followed Forest since 1961. My first away game in '65 at Hull City was postponed because of snow. My next game was at Old Trafford in '67, which was the season we came runners up in the League. I went to both games with my dad and after the match; a mob of Forest tried to take United's Strettford end. In those, days Forest's mob was made up of all sorts. We had quite a few greasers and bikers that followed the team. We had blokes like Scerm and Kenny Grease who led the lads. Kenny was famous for his siren call and when he did it we all knew that our top boys weren't far away. I remember Tottenham coming to Forest in the late 60s and loads of them had shaved heads and white boiler suits and steel toe capped boots. I stood there and laughed my bollocks off at them. Two weeks later I had my head shaved and had the big boots on. When I had my hair shaved off my mum nearly had a fit when I got home. "Jim" she shouted and called my dad to come and have a look. Over the years, I've met some real characters at football. I met Hickey from Chelsea when I was inside and we stayed friends for a long time afterwards. I knew Scarrett well and I know some of the Spurs lads. When I was about 14 I went with about 30 other Forest lads into Leicester's end when we were playing them, and I remember Leicester lining up on one side as we pushed through. Next thing I see this, what looked like a little white spot, coming towards me, and as it got nearer it got bigger and then whack, this golf ball hit me smack bang in the middle of the forehead and it nearly knocked me clean out. I was half carried out of their end and back in with the rest of the Forest fans in the away end. I didn't know what day of the week it was. I was out on my feet. Afterwards the Old Bill split Forest into two mobs and Leicester got behind both mobs and ran us everywhere all the way back to the station. But they've never ever done us since, at their place or in Nottingham, and that's the truth. In '79 I got badly stabbed and was only given 4 hours to live, so when I recovered I fucked off to America and came back full time 11 years later, and that's when I met Gary. He was one of the new breed of Forest faces with a completely different mentality to us 60s and 70s dinosaurs. If you don't put the

NAME: Skeeny
AGE: 49
CLUB: Nottingham Forest
JOB: Business Man

time and effort into getting to know Gary then it's your loss, you've missed something. He's a special type of bloke, a one off, and a top man. He's very reliable. The daftest thing he's ever done was to sell his match ticket for the Germany v England game in Munich when we won 5-1. I told him as soon as he done it he was going to miss something special, but he just looked at me with that daft grin and shrugged his shoulders. Typical Boatsy, he didn't care less.

First day at school, age 11.

Me and the boys, Skegness, early eighties.
(Sitting next to Scarrot)

Lifting that famous trophy.

Above: With the Firm, Anderlect, away 1984.

Left: Me and my best mate, 18th. birthday, outside Jersey's main boozer.

Below: Corfu, 1984.

Boys holiday,
Corfu 1984.

Nottingham Market
Square, summertime, no
football

Belfast 1987, away
with England.

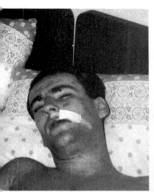

Morning after, Yugoslavia 1987, with England.

Belfast 1987, with John from sheff.

Glasgow 1987 (England).

Skegness, eighties.

Inside the Pudding Shop, Istanbul of *Midnight Express* fame.

The Pudding Shop, on the way to the England game.

Saturday, March 7, 1987   5

38 years for nine football hooligans

NINE soccer thugs were jailed for a total of 38 years yesterday for a deliberately-planned terror rampage on rival fans.

They hurled bricks and debris into vehicles trapped in traffic, injuring seven people, Nottingham Crown court heard.

Judge Keith Matthewman, QC, said: "This is one of the worst, if not the worst incident connected with football here.

Screaming

"People were terrorised by flying glass and being punched and kicked. Women and children were screaming in panic."

The nine—all Nottingham Forest supporters from the Nottingham area—attacked Everton fans after the game last year.

The nine—aged between 18 and 27—got individual terms ranging from three years to 5½ years for affray.

THE DAY 400-MAN TERROR CAME TO SQUARE

By ANDY BUCKLOW

POLICE have drawn up emergency plans to prevent a repeat of Nottingham's worst outbreak of hooliganism — when 400 people fought a pitched battle in the Old Market Square.

As the last of more than 60 youths were dealt with in court — 30 of them have now been jailed or given other custodial sentences — for their part in the mob warfare on June 23 last year, a senior officer involved in the case said: "We are determined to keep the city centre clear of hooligans."

He admitted that the police had been caught by surprise when hundreds of thugs from Nottingham, Derby and Leicester moved into the city on that Saturday evening last summer.

"We had no idea at all what was about to happen — that is why we were so outnumbered," he said.

'Rush for cover'

What happened in the Square sickened even officers used to policing highly-charged football matches.

Innocent bystanders had to rush for cover as bottles, glasses and roadside debris were hurled through the air.

A number of the youths were armed with knives and metal bars.

Women and children had to clamber aboard buses to escape, and traffic was brought to a standstill as the mob dispersed and engaged in running battles.

One man who had lived in Belfast said later: "It was worse than any trouble I have ever seen in Northern Ireland."

One small girl was so disturbed by what she saw that her mother later took her back to the scene to reassure her that such scenes were not commonplace in Nottingham.

The origins of the battle lay in the bitter rivalry between Forest and Derby County supporters.

The Derby hooligan element named themselves the DLF — Derby Lunatic Fringe — with the aim of causing disorder at football matches, particularly against Forest.

Retaliation

They allied with Leicester youths to form the Derby-Leicester Alliance.

Their trip to Nottingham was in retaliation for violent incidents when Nottingham youths visited Leicester earlier in the year.

But the Nottingham hoodlums had recruited a reception party.

When the DLA appeared in the Square, the Nottingham contingent poured out of nearby pubs.

At the outbreak of the violence there were just four policemen in the Square.

"During this time there was absolutely no control over what was taking place," said the police.

But even after the arrival of more officers, groups split up and chased each other round the streets.

Only six youths were arrested that night.

But police later tracked down a further 57, who have now all been sentenced by Guildhall magistrates.

Compliments
NOTTINGHAM FOREST
EXECUTIVE CREW
Away on business
Midlands No. 1 FIRM

FOREST

On the pitch at
Peterboro.

Our mob, Brussels
t Anderlect.

Our firm in London.

Two of our finest, Dale C. and Pele in Bruges, 1984.

CHAPTER 3

Sheepshaggers

'D NOW PACKED in my job at the market and decided to go out on the knocker with a few of the lads from football. I signed on the dole and went around the country selling ironing board covers, tea towels and flannels, door to door. A few of the lads claimed they could earn up to £150 a day. We'd go off to somewhere like Torquay for a week and come back loaded with money. We'd travel to all parts of the country in a minibus. Several blokes in Nottingham were running this type of racket. They gave you the stock and took, like, 40 per cent of what you sold. They'd also put you up in digs and paid for that to. They were on a right good earner and were making more money than anyone else I knew. If it was pissing down with rain or things weren't selling well for one reason or another, we'd turn it in for the day and we'd go off to the nearest pub, have a couple of pints and have a look around at what we could thieve. We'd do the fruit machines, the fag machines and if there was one in the men's toilet, we'd even do the condom machine. We'd get the cash boxes out by forcing them open with a screwdriver, a real easy job. We'd earn lots of money down south, mostly in the affluent areas like Bournemouth, Weymouth, Southampton, and Chichester. Most of the machines only had two small bolts holding the cash tray in so it was bang, bang, grab the money and we're gone. It was as I say so, so easy.

Just before I left the market we had a pre-arranged row with Derby in Nottingham. It was one of the Derby lads' birthday so we knew they was coming to us but the rumour going around was that they were joining up with Leicester and were calling themselves the D.L.A., which stood for the Derby Leicester Alliance. By 6 oclock on the night, we had a massive mob waiting for them in Yates pub, the football season was'nt even on as it was June but we had a firm and a half out waiting for them.

We sent some scouts down to the train station to watch for their arrival. There were no coppers about, and as far as we knew, they knew nothing about it. The excitement and buzz around the place was unbelievable. A few of the older lads were going around everybody trying to keep everyone calm. People were getting fidgety and wanted some action. Pubs on the other side of the square were jammed packed with lads, all up for it. At about seven o'clock, the scouts came running back and we knew the opposition were here. About 120 of them came across the square towards us and it looked good. There was only two coppers strolling across the square on normal duties and they were unaware of what was seconds away from happening. It was still relatively early so there were no Saturday evening revellers out yet. Right outside the pub there was road works going on so there was lots of weapons and ammo on offer if needed.

They came bowling across the square looking as if they were up for it and we just stormed out towards them. They were surrounded as we came at them from every direction. It went toe-to-toe for a minute and then they got swamped and over-ran. Then it was time for them to run, as we gave chase, and they then split and ran in all directions. There was little pockets of fighting going on down side alleys and side roads but the majority of them fucked off back up the road towards Derby, but for an hour after the old Bill had restored some order there were still skirmishes going on in various parts of the city centre. They got mullered by us but they still say they had a result against us. For the life of me, I can't see how. Why did they come with Leicester? Why not come on their own? It's like us lot joining up with Stoke City to go to Derby. We wouldn't do it. It seemed that they were that scared of us that they needed the support of another club to take us on. Even to this day they deny the Derby Leicester Alliance and say they know nothing about it, which is total bollocks. On the night, the police managed to put what was left of Derby and Leicester back onto trains and buses. There was a few bodies lying out cold on the floor and it took the Old Bill a good two hours to restore complete order. On the night, there was probably around ten arrests but a week later 70 houses were raided.

They came to my house a while after but I was, luckily, out at work, and left a message for me to get in touch with them. I knew it would only be a matter of time before they caught up with me so I went to the police station with my solicitor. I was interviewed and charged with threatening behaviour but they never had any evidence. There must have been six to seven hundred people in that square; there was no C.C.T.V. and no photographic evidence. I was only 19 and a young lad, and admitted to watching the fight from the pub, but the coppers said that was good enough for a threatening behaviour charge. In their eyes, they saw me as guilty. In court, we had a three-week trial along with the Derby lads who had also been dawn raided and charged with threatening behaviour. To be honest we all thought we'd get off with it as the police evidence was so flimsy. Surely, it wouldn't and couldn't stand up in court? or would it? Out of the 60 in court, 30 of us received prison sentences. I got 100 days in North Sea Youth Detention Centre. I also had three other charges to be taken into consideration. I'd been in a fight a few weeks before and had put my hand through a glass window. I'd also been charged with pulling a knife on a bouncer outside a nightclub but the charges against me were dropped on that one, but I did get an extra 7 days for the window and another 7 days for something else, so all in all I'd been sentenced to three and a half months. The place I was off to was run on a military boot camp basis with the emphasis on the short, sharp, shock treatment. You had to quick-march everywhere and stand to attention when not marching. Thing is I couldn't march. All you could hear was the screws shouting, "Get in line Clarke, keep in time Clarke". I was hopeless at marching.

When I first got there all eight of us that had been sent there had our heads shaved like skinheads minus the Doc Martens, flight jackets and jeans at half-mast. I was in there with Tommo from Derby who to this day is still a good mate of mine, and Ashley Green from Leicester and we all just bonded and became great mates who looked out for one another. If the truth, be known we were right cocky young fuckers. One day I was laughing and joking with someone and this screw walks over, slaps me around the face and tells me to "shut the fuck up and behave myself, sit down over there and you call me sir". You had to polish ya boots until you could see your face in the shine. Ten of us would sleep in a dorm and there was a lot of bullying in there but early on, I banged a few people so our lot was left well alone.

We were woken at 6.00 a.m. everyday and then we had a quick two minutes to wash and clean our teeth. We were then marched back into the dorm at the double. All you could hear was "left right left right", and then you had to fold your bed blankets up and lay them at one end of the bed for inspection. If all was O.K. you were marched off for breakfast and then it was more marching and square bashing outside. Me and Tommo landed cushy jobs outside in the gardens. We used to cut the grass or do the weeding. It was a welcome relief from going everywhere at 100 mph with your arms swinging at your sides like piston rods, plus it gave you the chance to breathe in some fresh air and not have the smell of piss and bleach and over-cooked cabbage attacking your nostrils. On the garden duties, we had an old screw who knew the score, and as long as you did as you were told and did your work he didn't bother you. He was like Mr. Barrowclough in the T.V. programme Porridge. You had to earn your privileges in there and if you became a red-band then that entitled you to watch T.V. a couple of nights a week. It didn't last long for me because after two days of earning, I had a row with a screw and my telly watching days were over.

Every Sunday you had a 4-mile run around the camp. I only did it once and came 7th out of 150 lads, but it wasn't for me and I got out of it by doing a bit of overtime on the gardening to get more money. Some days when it was hot, we'd take our blue prison jackets and tee shirts off and laze about in the sun getting tanned. You had a blue and white striped shirt for best but you had no where to go when you had your best kit on so it was all a bit pointless. We'd do a bit of work and when Mr. Barrowclough wasn't looking, or he'd popped off for a quick smoke, we'd down tools and lay about sunbathing. When I got out and back home I was as fit as fuck, what with the gardening, the prison gym and a healthy, glowing tan. A few people, who didn't know where I'd been, would ask if I'd been away on holiday. "Well, a holiday of sorts", I'd reply!

Some people in there just couldn't take it, what with the bullying and the screws shouting and bawling in your face, and the grub. Some kids would break down in floods of tears and would become trembling, nervous wrecks. No one bothered us lot though. They just thought we were nutty football hooligans and gave us a wide berth. One scummy burglar from Rotherham tried it on one day and I just flipped and gave him a couple of whacks and slammed him, by the throat, into a door. He shit himself and backed down. If you did have a grievance with someone then normally it got sorted out, one on to one, in the boot room. People have asked me if I think it done me good. One day I remember a screw telling me that 90 per cent of us lot in there would end up in adult prisons. For me I went another 20 years before, unfortunately, it came true.

The experience in there gave me a kick up the arse and I learned a lot. To be honest I quite liked the army type way of life. How many of the other 400 kids doing time in there could say that, I don't know. The discipline was something I was missing in my everyday life and I didn't regret getting sent there not one bit. I've made some lifelong friends from being in there, even though some of them are Derby County fans, but then again all Forest and Derby fans love to hate one another. They're geographically our nearest rivals but on the other hand, just up the road is Mansfield, but it's the complete opposite to Derby and we have no problem with Mansfeild and despite a few minor differences between individuals we get on great with most of their boys. We go to some of their big games and they come over to some of ours. On their day, they can pull some serious numbers and have a game firm. Ask any team in the lower leagues and they'll tell you about Mansfield, plus they've got a big following at England games, and in their ranks they have Palmer who claims to be Britain's best looking football hooligan! But then again that's debatable. Mansfield's main rivals are Lincoln and the two teams have had some right rows over the years, believe me, Lincoln can be a right dodgy place to go of a night. Go there, looking for a row and I guarantee you'll find it. The whole town will turn out at the first sign of trouble. If I went over to Derby for a night out, there would be a good chance I'd get some grief. The same thing is true of the girls when they go out. You don't get many going for a night out in Derby and vice versa. The same as following the football teams, you don't get many people from Derby following Forest and I don't know anyone from Nottingham that would wear a Derby shirt in Nottingham. They'd get told to take it off or get a slap. You see the odd Man Utd or Liverpool or Chelsea shirt, but that would only be during the day time when people are out shopping; you wouldn't see it of a night time in the bars and pubs. Some of the border towns and villages like Ilkeston, are half and half and for most of the year suffer one another, but come match days they kick the fuck out of one another. The place is a one-horse town and has a close- knit community. If they don't know ya face there's a good chance you could get a slap. It's a naughty little town. The National Front once had their headquarters there and you don't see many black and Asian faces around there.

NAME: John
AGE: 38
CLUB: Sheffield United
JOB: C.N.C. Setter/Operator

I've known Gary for going on 20 years now. From where I used to live on the outskirts of Sheffield. We used to go to Skegness for the weekend and on this particular day me and me mate were just having a walk around town, just taking things in, when we saw these 30 or so lads walking about. We just tagged on to the back of them and overheard them talking about doing some skinheads. "That'll do us," we were thinking. We found out later that these boys were from Nottingham and they were part of the young Forest Casuals. They called them- selves Shadies or something or other. They were on the lookout for skinheads from Boston and they told us they had fights with them every time they were in town. They looked in a pub where these skins sometimes hung out, but the place was empty. These Forest lads were a mixture of ages but Gary seemed to be the one they all listened to. He seemed to have a presence about him. We got chat- ting to them all and felt quiet comfortable and safe with them. There was only two of us so we knew they weren't the type to turn on us, we could just tell. I'd met a few Forest lads who were with them that day a couple of years before, and they remembered me, so that's how it all progressed.

A couple of weeks later Forest played West Ham in a night match at the City ground and four of us drove down from Sheffield in a van to go to the game with Gary and the rest of the lads. From there we progressed on to going to England games together. I remember we played Scotland down at Wembley, and Gary came in the mini-bus with us and we nearly ended up fighting with a Stoke mob. It was crazy as there was Jocks everywhere and little mobs of English milling about and we nearly end up fighting one another. I said to these lads "come on lads there's plenty of Jocks to fight, why are we arguing amongst ourselves?" These lads were a lot older than we were as we were just kids but these were proper men. Anyway, it calmed down and they walked off, and a few of the lads I was with ended up going to one of them Soho peep shows. I could hear a bit of a commotion going on outside and then I heard someone shout "they're here." I went running out into the street with the rest of the lads and got stuck into, these tartan-clad clowns, then I got hit on the head with a brick one of them had thrown, that was me out of the game. That was my first recollection of going to an England game with Boatsy. The thing with Forest and Sheffield Utd I've tended to stay out of it due to my friendship with Gary but Forest, when they come to Sheffield, always come early and stay late drinking in the Penny Black pub.

CHAPTER 4

The Battle of Maid Marion

M Y CAREER, work wise, changed course when I landed a job at Boots warehouse. Boots is one of the biggest employers in Nottingham. When I was there, they employed around 11,000 people from the Nottingham area alone and it was a bit of a cushy job. I had a job driving the forklift and stuff like that. We had a discount shop, which was cheap, and you could buy bundles of gear for next to nothing. It was shift work but the money was good so it kept me out of trouble for a while.

Everton at home was our last home game of the 85/86 season. A mini-bus load of Scouse lads jumped out and started fighting in the street with some of our lads and because we were all spread out, they didn't realise just how many of us there was. Everyone's seen what's going on and attacked those from the bus. We smashed them to pieces and they couldn't get away because they were stuck in traffic. A few cars with Everton fans were also targeted and Forest fans went on the rampage all the way down the Maid Marion Way. We all fucked off before the Old Bill turned up but word on the street was they knew who they were looking for and I was one of the usual suspects. I went to see my solicitor who advised me just to keep my head down and keep out of the way for a while.

The cops turned up at my house a couple of times and I was either out or didn't answer the door, and for a few days I stayed at a bird's house, over in Clifton.

The following Saturday, the last game of the season, we had Oxford United away. It was a nothing game with us just above mid-table. A few of us went down for the game, and we found out that Oxford's mob and a few local black lads were drinking in a pub called The Paradise. We were just about to hit it with some distress flares that one of the lads had pinched from a camping shop, when as he took aim at the pub the Nottingham C.I.D. who I had no idea was there leapt on me and nicked me. I was taken to Oxford police station and after the game was taken by police car back to Nottingham. I was interviewed over the weekend and then on the Monday, I was charged with affray and given bail, gradually over the course of weeks, the charge was dropped to a lesser charge of threatening behaviour.

At the trial in Nottingham some of our lads got some serious bird. A couple of the lads got 5 years. The Scouse lads that started it got away scot-free. They made out they were the innocent party and were attacked after the game whilst caught up in traffic. Some of our lot were still being picked out and picked up six months after the event. I got my case thrown out of court after 5 or 6 days of the hearing. The prosecution claimed that I was seen throwing bricks at the van and attacking the Everton fans inside. That was total bollocks. My events of that day were so different. I told the court that after the game I walked through town and went for a drink, and denied I was anywhere near the incident. There was no C.C.T.V. or photographic evidence but I'd been grassed up by a snake of a cunt who told police "that Boatsy had led his mob up Maid Marian Way and attacked the Everton fans". When he was summoned to appear in court he retracted his state-ment, funny that aint it? I was now, I suppose, the top boy of my age group and was getting a bit of a reputation as a bit of a nutter.

We were playing Derby County at home and because we'd been to prison with a few of their lads, the aggro between us lot had sort of died out, plus we hadn't played them for a few years, but on the day of the game that didn't stop 200 of our lads having an early meet down near the canal. We were standing outside one of the pubs down there when a car pulled up alongside us. Inside were four of Derby's boys, one of them lent out of the window and spoke. "Look lads, if you want it we're drinking in The Meadows," A few of the lads wanted to do the blokes in the car but because we had no coppers with us we kept our cool and split up into two 100 strong firms to go to the pub where they claimed they were drinking. The Meadows is about a mile away from the ground, and is a bit of a rough housing estate and is way off the beaten track for away fans coming into Nottingham. We navigated the side streets and back streets of the estate without a single copper on our case. Scarrett and a few of the lads casually walked up to the pub and looked in the windows. The pub was deserted, it was still only midday and inside was just one old codger drinking a pint of smooth with a roll up dangling from his lower lip. A few lads who'd been having a scout around come running back, excitedly. They'd found where they were drinking, and it was a pub on a corner in amongst rows of terraced houses like on Coronation Street. We headed towards the pub where one mob came from one direction and put all the windows in and the rest of the lads came from the other way and used an axe to get the barracked door open and get inside the pub within seconds the place was smashed to smithereens. All the Derby boys inside had heard what was going on outside and had run down into the cellar and locked themselves in. Somebody pinched the till with all the takings in it. The landlord, along with his staff and a few regulars, ran upstairs and hid. As soon as we heard the sirens, we were off and disappeared into the alleyways and back roads of the estate. That night the scene was shown on local T.V. and the place was a complete wreck.

About a week later I'm thinking I'd got away with it when my gaffer at work came into the warehouse at Boots and told me that the police would like to talk to me over at the office. That was it. They cautioned me with all the "anything you may say" bollocks and then led me away in handcuffs. I was so embarrassed and I think I might have even gone bright red. What must have the office girls thought? I knew that the police had gone a bit over the top by coming to get me dressed head to toe in their riot gear. A couple of them were even carrying the Perspex riot shields. The Old Bill kept me for 24 hours but all I'd say to their questions was "no comment". They were all right but I could tell they were getting the right hump. They charged me with suspicion of riot and tried to get me to do an I.D. parade, which I refused. But on the Monday I had to report back to the police station where they done one of them personal I.D. parades where you have a copper either side of you and they bring in whoever it is to see if they can identify you. They can see you through a glass panel, but you can't see them. The Old Bill had bought in three of Derby's main lads to I.D. me. One of them, Smithy, who was a van driver, was brought in still wearing his delivery uniform. They'd dragged him in straight from work. The police had caught the Derby lot cowering in the cellar when they arrived so they had to give statements to the cops. They were also threatened that if they didn't name names then they would face some serious charges and some serious bird went with these charges. Scarrett's name, came up quite a lot and he was arrested and spent a year inside on remand. The three Derby lads they brought in to pick me out also said that I wasn't there so all the charges against me were dropped.

All in all there was five of us arrested and one of our lads got jail for 4 years. The Derby lads never talk about that row. Perhaps it's an embarrassment to them. A few of them lot must have had a long, hard look at themselves. It's one thing hiding in a pub cellar frightened out of your life, but it's another when you grass up a fellow combatant.

One Saturday Notts County were playing Spurs, I think in the F.A. Cup. Forest had been knocked out or didn't have a game. I was just on the piss around near the station and I bumped into Ashley Green who I'd been in North Sea Camp with, and a mate of his, Jonno from Leicester. We had a few drinks and they invited me back to Leicester to carry on the session down there. I wasn't sure if that was a good move.

"Come on, you'll be alright", they said.

I still wasn't convinced but like a daft cunt I got talked into it, and jumped on the train with them down to Leicester. It was about 7.30 p.m. and the train was quite busy as it was carrying on through to London. On board was 15-20 Spurs fans that had been to the game at County. They started getting a bit loud and a few of them started gobbing off at people around them, including us three who had just been sitting there minding our own business. Words were exchanged and the next minute the whole train is in uproar. I'm at the front standing in the gangway so there's no room for them to overrun us and it's basically, one-to-one with no room for dancing. From Loughborough to Leicester it was non-stop fighting.

When we pulled into Leicester station my eye is black and swollen where I've taken a solid right-hander. The Old Bill come on board as the train stops and the transport police arrest me as soon as I step onto the platform.

"He's one of them, he's one of them" as the Yids turn dirty and point me out. I'm taken off and charged with threatening behaviour. About a month after the event I get a letter through the post with a whole host of new charges being brought against me. On there is affray, malicious wounding and three counts of A.B.H. and there I was willing to plead guilty to the original charge of threatening behaviour. After 18 months it finally went to trial at Leicester Crown Court and surprise, surprise, all these Tottenham lads turned up to appear as witnesses against me. I couldn't believe it. They were as guilty as me, more so in fact. They'd caused the whole fucking thing and now they were standing up in court talking absolute bollocks. One of them even stood up and said he'd had his face slashed but that he didn't go to hospital to have his wounds tended to, instead he went to his own G.P. who stitched him up with butterfly stitches at his local surgery. He probably cut himself shaving. The only cunt getting stitched up was me! The evidence was so dodgy it was almost laughable. I looked at the Judge and the jury a few times and I could see them shaking their heads and trying not to smile as some of these people unfolded a total pack of lies. I had a brilliant barrister that my solicitor had hired from London and he went and spoke to the Judge when the court was adjourned. The barrister then came back to me and went over the conversation he'd had with the Judge who had said that he didn't really want to listen to certain people telling blatant lies and if I pleaded guilty to affray he would give me a 9 month sentence. However, if the trial carried on and the jury found me guilty then I could receive a three-year jail term, so I went "guilty" and back into court we went. Straight away he dropped all the other charges and then gave me a twelve-month prison sentence. "You bastard" I thought. "Suspended for 12 months," he added with a pause. A smile lit up the whole of my face. The coppers were not best pleased and were still going mad outside the court. I couldn't believe it. I'd got away with it, and I swore that now I was going to leave off the booze and keep out of trouble.

NAME: Arthur
AGE: 43
CLUB: Nottingham Forest

My first game was against York in the old Second Division in 1972, and I went with my dad. The most memorable game ever for me was Birmingham away a few years back. We'd played Birmingham at the City ground earlier that season and they'd brought 80 lads in a right tight firm. We had no one out that day because most of the lads were away on a stag do for the weekend. We'd played Birmingham a few times and they'd never really shown up, so because they'd come to us we decided to repay the compliment for the game down at their place. I give them their due, when they came to Nottingham the 30 lads we did have out knew they were facing a top firm. We were drinking on the Meadows estate in The Poets Corner pub and they found us. They came down a side street and someone shouted "they're here." We came bowling out, no Old Bill and it kicked off, but fair play to them, they run us back into the pub. We held them in the doorway with a few of our lads waving pool cues about, and when the Old Bill arrived it all calmed down, so the trip down there was a bit of a revenge mission. If they could come to us, we could go to them. We've had a bit of a history with them. We turned them over in the F.A. Cup five or six years previously.

One of our lads sorted out a pub about 2 miles from their ground in a place called Sparkbrooke, which was on an estate. A couple of the lads had been down a few weeks before and had a scout about. So most of us travelled down on the morning of the game. That's what the Forest lads usually do for an away game, travel by car, we're well known for it. A few of us left together but most got there in dribs and drabs. The pub was on a rough looking, run down council estate. When we got there at midday the place was deserted. Four of us went into the pub and the other fella who was with us, who aint one of the lads, moved the car out of the way. A few car loads of the Forest lads from Stapleford were sat drinking at the bar and very quickly the pub began to fill up, and in no time we had 60 to 70 lads in there. We were expecting loads more and word was that more were on their way. As far as I know, no one by this stage had been on to Birmingham to let them know we were here. I looked around and saw a few of our main faces and the rest of the lads looked confident so I felt if it came on top we would do well. One of our lads, who'd been outside drinking, walked in and shouted that Birmingham were here. I was having a drink in the pool- room at the time and for a second found it hard to believe that Birmingham had turned up, seeing as we were in a pub, in the middle of nowhere. We came out the pub and coming towards us, spread across the road, were 80 Birmingham lads. There was blacks and all sorts mixed in with them and most of them were tooled up to fuck. We had the bottles, glasses and pool balls so we just ran straight into them. We blasted them with our ammo and then it went hand to hand, and then we ran them 100 yards to the top of the road, where some of them stopped and had a bit of a go.

The fighting had now spread out and we were on a crossroads with some of them and us going left and some going right. There's still no Old Bill as we chase the stragglers off into the distance and we think that's it, they won't be back as we walk back to the pub in dribs and drabs. Out of a side road come 50 Birmingham. We've all spread out now so 3 or 4 of us go towards them and start fighting with 3 black lads at the front. A couple of them are waving bits of fencing, with nails sticking out, at us. They're big lads and are as game as fuck. I'm standing fighting and avoiding the wood and the nails, when I'm hit on the back of the head by a flying brick. I stop fighting and I'm now on automatic pilot as I stagger off, barely able to stand upright. My head's spinning and I'm not totally in control of my legs. I look around and I realise I'm now 150 yards away from the rest of our lads. I stagger back towards the pub and from around a corner come 3 lads. One of them pulls a knife out on me and the other lads grab my arms and try to hold me still. "Fuck me," I'm thinking, "I'm going to die." The Asian looking bloke lunges at me and I smack him one but he manages to slash my wrist as he goes flying backwards and his two mates let go of me, unsure of what to do. I break free and try to run off but all I can manage is a wobbly fast walk. I head back towards the bulk of our lot who are still fighting up ahead of me. I turn the corner near the pub and some more black lads appear. One of them bounces up and down in front of me and I put my hands up to protect myself and bang, he hits me in the face and I'm unconscious. What happens next I've no idea. I'm out cold but people told me afterwards what happens next. The fighting's been going on for 15 to 20 minutes and still no police have arrived. It didn't take much for the black geezer to knock me out. I think the brick on the back of the head a few minutes earlier done most of the damage. As I'm laid out on the floor, a couple of them pick up a concrete slab and slam it down on the top of my head. They also stick the boot in but I can't feel or remember anything. The Forest lads have seen what's going on with me, and come charging back up the road and back these geezers off and protect me by standing around me. I wake up still on the floor and covered in claret. I don't know where I am but I remember a copper and a paramedic kneeling down next to me and asking me what my name was, but I can't remember it. They then ask me where I'm from and one of our lot, as quick as a flash, said "he's from Brick Lane," and I remember laughing at that. Next thing they fit a neck brace to me and take me to hospital where I have 40 stitches in my head wound. They wanted to keep me in over night but I got one of the lads, who's come in the ambulance with me, to pick me up and take me home after I'd discharged myself. My head was just killing me and I'm thinking I've had better days than this, but I just had to get home no matter how bad I was. There was no way I was staying in a hospital miles from home. When I was dropped off my wife was not happy. She was concerned I would slip into a coma or something. She was panicking, and really worried and I tried my best to reassure her that I was all right. I somehow managed to sleep that night but the next morning I was awoken by the telephone ringing. I'm feeling battered and bruised and my head is a little tender. I pick up the phone. "Hello." A voice at the other end mutters, "don't mess with the Blues," and puts the phone down. I can't believe it and stand there, stunned. "Where the fuck's that come from?" I'm thinking. "How the fuck had that cheeky cunt got my number?" That call did my head in. I did the 1471 and I got the number, and it was as I thought a Birmingham number. I pulled a few strings and found out the number was a public telephone box not far from New Street. I never did find out who made that call or how they got hold of my home number. Did they get it from somebody at the hospital? The police? Or did we have a grass in the camp? I wonder.

A few days later the police turned up and want me to make a statement, which I refused to do. Both Nottingham and Birmingham police were investigating the incident but I told them very little. To me if you dish it out you've got to be able to take it when it comes your way. It's as simple as that.
The following year we caught hold of a mob of them outside the City ground and we smashed them all over the place. We fucked them big time. I've been around football violence for 20 years but what happened to me was out of order. What's the old saying? What goes around comes around. I think that may well be true. Watch this space. The fella who punched me in the face I'd probably happily have a drink with, but the cunts who dropped the slab on my head, well that's just bang out of order. That's wrong and you can't get away from that. I'd love to meet them again and one day I just might.

CHAPTER 5

My England Debut

PAUL SCARRETT was a regular on the England International scene. He came back to Nottingham with the most amazing stories about him and Hickey and the rest of the Chelsea lads who at the time were the top faces at England games. I wanted to go to loads of England games, like out to Mexico, but I just couldn't afford it. I just couldn't raise the finances. Eventually I had my money coming in from the job at Boots so I thought, "fuck it, I'm going to go to the England v Scotland game." I was good mates with a Sheffield United lad named John. I first met up with him in Skegness and we have stayed mates ever since. He invited me over to watch Sheffield United play Leeds on a Tuesday night and he told me there was a vanload of them going down to London to watch the England game at Wembley. I took two days off work, and went and met up with John in Sheffield. United had a massive mob of about 300 out for that Leeds game but Leeds failed to show and it was a bit of an anti-climax.

Early the next morning John and the rest of the lads picked me up on the way down to Wembley, as soon as we got into central London and parked up we had, running battles with the Jocks around Soho. I loved it. It was my first taste of being on England duty with firms from other clubs. I'd managed to blag myself a ticket for the game and was well pleased, that was until I realised I was in the Scotland section on my own. There was tartan everywhere and I was surrounded by Jocks, plus I stood out like a spare prick at a wedding. I was dressed in a ski coat with a hood and had nothing check or tartan on. A bloke standing behind in the crowd me taps me on the shoulder and asks me the time. I look around and hundreds of eyes are staring at me waiting for my reply. I'm not that daft a cunt so I just shrugged my shoulders and didn't answer. Next thing I know my hood's pulled up over my head, I'm being dragged down backwards onto the deck, and I'm being kicked down the terraces. A copper 'as seen what's going on and quickly picks me up and drags me out of it.

"What the fuck are you doing in here you daft prick?" he asks, and with that, he leads me into the England section. All that old shit that the Jocks don't cause trouble at football and the Tartan Army are a friendly bunch is all bollocks. They would have killed me. Afterwards we all made our way back to the mini-bus with no trouble and the lads dropped me back in Nottingham.

My next taste of an England game was a trip out to Spain. I was still working at Boots and bumped into Scarrett in town one night who told me that Chubby Chris Henderson, one of the Chelsea lads, was running a bus out to Madrid for the Spain v England game. Scarrett was drumming up as many Forest lads as he could for the trip. I had a sneaky look at the holiday rota in work and it looked full up so I opted to have a few days on the sick. The game was on a Wednesday night but the coach was leaving from Fulham Broadway on the Sunday night. Chris charged £50 per person. On board were eight of us from Nottingham, there were five lads from Darlington and all the rest were Chelsea boys. We got across the Channel relatively hassle-free and our first real stop was in Paris. Gez Mullen, one of ours, was arrested for doing a large one on a pool table, a couple of the Chelsea lads got nicked, and while all this was going on Scarrett was up to his usual tricks. The next port of call was Burgos, which is just over the French border into Spain. We got there on the Tuesday night and had planned to watch the England under 21s play against the Spanish under 21s but we caused a riot in the local disco and a few locals got bashed up and one was stabbed in the arm. Giles, one of the Chelsea lads, was dressed in shorts and Sombrero hat but it was February and fucking freezing, but he didn't care. When the fight started in the disco someone let off some C.S. gas and people were spluttering and staggering out the doors to get some fresh air. We all fucked off back to the coach well pissed and in need of some sleep.

We woke the next morning with the inside of the windows covered in a frost and with all of us freezing our bollocks off. Someone wiped the window over with their sleeve so that we could see a bit of day- light and standing outside surrounding the coach was what looked like the entire police forces of Burgos and northern Spain. With them was a load of blokes with bandages around their heads, arms in slings, cut lips and black eyes. We were ordered off the coach one at a time and told to line up. I'm thinking to myself that I'm bound to be picked out knowing my luck but to my surprise I never got the dreaded tap on the shoulder. Two lads from Nottingham were arrested and one Chelsea lad. They were held in a Spanish jail for two weeks until money was sent out for them to be released. A mate of mine Johnny Cotton from Clifton was one of those held and he said it was a nightmare. The rest of us were put back on the coach and were told basically to, "Fuck off out of town."

We're now off minus a few of the lads and we have a two-hour drive down to Madrid, where we eventually arrive around lunchtime. We're straight into the first bar we see, and get totally pissed. When we come out and head for the stadium, we realise just how cold it is. There's no trouble outside the stadium but the Spanish Old Bill, eye us with suspicion. Inside we're standing on a terrace with the Spanish in a section above us, a steady stream of warm piss comes down on us from above some of it is coming through the cracks in the concrete, but some Spanish are just pissing over the top onto us down below. I wasn't impressed by the attitude of the local Old Bill who just laughed when we pointed out what was going on above us. The ground itself was a right shit hole and was in need of some money spent on it. There was only about 500 England fans in total out there with our coach the only group of real lads. When we came out of the game at the final whistle, which England won 4-0 with all four goals coming from Gary Lineker, we turned left out of the stadium and out onto a busy street, just up ahead of us was what looked like a mob of Spanish and by their body language they were looking for a row. Between them and us were just a couple of coppers who, to tell you the truth, didn't look that interested.

"Get into them," shouted one of the Chelsea boys as the Spanish threw bricks and bottles at us.

"Stay together," said a cockney voice to my right as we walked purpose-fully towards them. A roar went up, on our side, and we steamed straight into them and with the first punch thrown, we'd scattered them everywhere across the car park. I give that Chelsea lot their due. They were as game as fuck and didn't give a shit for anyone. The Spanish Old Bill weren't too pleased with our little spat so drew their batons and rounded us up, put us on the bus and escorted us out of Madrid. Still it got every-ones hearts pumping and the little bit of action warmed us all up. We were soon on the motorway and heading back towards Burgos and I was sure a warm, friendly welcome from the locals. By now we've all well fucked and some of us haven't had proper nights sleep for days. I feel dirty when I've not bathed or showered, all I've had is a quick cat's lick around my face, and a tooth-brush quickly brushed across my teeth, which by now feel and look like green suede. In between bouts of nodding off and frequently telling Scarrett to shut up and get some sleep, I can see there's a blizzard going on outside. The snow is settling on the road and you can hardly see anything out the windows as the coach is bombing along the motorway in the darkness.

I must have dozed back off because the next minute there's a loud bang and we seemed to have come to a halt. I can feel blood coming from my nose and the cold night air hits me as snowflakes settle on my shoulder and I'm covered in broken glass. I still don't know what's happened. Am I dreaming? I look around me trying to figure out what's happened? and with the back of my hand, I wipe the blood away, which is seeping from my nose. My first thoughts are is that we'd been attacked and the windows had been bricked in. At that time, Spanish farmers were hijacking foreign lorries and bricking them, and setting them on fire in a protest about something or other. Those that could walk staggered off the bus in the darkness. I could hear people groaning and crying out for help. I've never felt so frightened and helpless in my life, these are the times when you'd wished you'd learned first aid. It turns out a lorry had parked up in the inside lane with no lights on and we'd ploughed straight into the back of it and on impact the coach had near on been ripped in half. The coach driver had seen the lorry at the very last second through the sleet and snow, swerved to miss him and clipped his rear end. The bus driver and a Chelsea lad had to be cut out of the wreckage. He was sat directly behind the driver and was in a coma for six months. The driver, sadly, lost both of his legs but if it hadn't been for his quick reactions and quick thinking it didn't bear thinking about what could have happened to the rest of us.

Those of us that could move, ran in the dark to the back of the coach to try to stop any traffic ploughing into the back of us. Someone shouted that someone was dead. Shock was now setting in on some people and others just sat there with their heads in their hands like Zombies. It took the emergency services an hour to get to us and we were all taken to hospital in a fleet of ambulances. There was nothing wrong with Scarrett but as usual, he pulled a fast one and made out he was more badly injured than he was. He was determined to milk it for all it was worth. Those that didn't stay in hospital were put up in a hotel in Burgos. While staying there, we ran up a bill up of about £3,000 on drinks and meals, but the Spanish authorities refused to pay it so the coppers were now threatening to nick us unless we paid up. A mob of locals had heard we were back in town and started congregating outside and they weren't there to give blood for the crash victims, they were there to take ours. The situation was turning nasty and the vigilante mob got bigger as news spread around town that the English that had caused trouble were now back in town and lording it up in a top hotel at the expense of the Spanish taxpayer. So we were now under police guard as the row about the unpaid bill rumbled on. The insurance people refused to pay it and the British Embassy also refused to pay it without certain guarantees. The Sun newspaper offered to pay as the hotel soon became overrun with reporters from all over Europe. We even had a local Nottingham reporter turn up to get our side of the story and wanting to interview the Forest lads and take some pictures for the paper. I wanted fuck all to do with it. I was off work on the sick and it was the last thing I needed. Scarrett never the less done every interview he could and back home we had television crews going around people's houses in Nottingham trying to talk to their families. It was total bollocks.

I phoned my mum and told her not to talk to anyone and not to give my name. I was more worried about my job at Boots and what my governors would think.

Eventually we were taken by train to the British Embassy in Madrid who were less than helpful and would not help fund us to get home, so we refused to leave the building unless they did help us. We explained we had nowhere to stay, we had no money and no transport home, and so we needed help. The Spanish authorities even threatened to nick the coach driver because they somehow felt he might have been partly responsible for the crash, which was total bollocks.

Eventually we did get home but I refused to do a 24-hour coach journey home and good old grandma paid for a flight home for me.

Chubby Chris in his book "Who Wants It", goes into more detail about the event and as far as I can remember he has some clippings from newspapers who went as far as to say that we were nothing but thugs and should have died in the snow. What's the old quote? "Never let the truth get in the way of a good story?" It seems that way doesn't it?

NAME: SCRIVS
AGE: 39
CLUB: Nottingham Forest

It was an F.A. Cup game, and it was the first time Forest had ever played on a Sunday and we beat Man City 4-1. That day Forest's Duncan McKenzie was out of this world. City's team was packed with stars like Mike Summerbee, Colin Bell, Francis Lee, Rodney Marsh and Dennis Law but McKenzie destroyed them. He tore them to pieces. That was in the 1973-74 season and we were in the old Second Division. Me dad took me to that game and he was a massive Forest fan. I first met the Forest lads through my mate Ginger, when I was 14 and was still at school. I first got nicked at Aston Villa when I was 15. I was just a kid and was with the Forest legend, Paul Scarrett who was a legend in my eyes.

CHAPTER 6

Welcome to Hell?
Land of the Donner

M E AND MY MATE, John from Sheffield, flew from Gatwick airport to Delamane in Turkey and from there we travelled down to Bodrum where we found an apartment for £1 each a night. We were out there for the European Championship qualifier to be played further along the coast in Izmir. Loads of people I'd met on my previous England trip were out there and by the look of it, the Chelsea lads were running the show as usual. Jock, Martin, Linky, Binman and Salford were all out there and had been on the infamous coach trip to Madrid. They were a great set of lads who treated us Forest lads with the utmost respect.

On the morning of the game we caught a bus for the hour and a half trip to Izmir. We hooked up with loads of other England lads and settled in one particular restaurant type bar, where we were on the piss all day. One of the Chelsea lads came up with the plan to fuck off without paying the bill, but give the money to the slowest one amongst and then if he gets caught all he's got to do is pay the bill. As simple as that, funny the things you do and plan to do when you've been on the booze all day. I know it was daft but anyway we've all got up and belted up the road, about ten of us being pursued by Turkish waiters in white shirts, black pressed trousers and shiny leather shoes. We ran lungs nearly bursting up the promenade and put a bit of distance between us and them, but when I took a look over my shoulder, one person amongst us, poor old Brady Dave a Chelsea fan from Bradford, was lagging well behind and was just yards from being caught. We'd given the money to Dave because he looked the most likely to be caught on the dash for freedom. He was the oldest and looked the most unfit, and our choice proved correct as he was soon surrounded by angry Turkish bar staff, frogmarched back to the restaurant and forced to turn his pockets out.

From there the rest of us made our way to the stadium which was a big, concrete, open bowl with no atmosphere. We stayed in there for ten minutes bored out of our brains before we decided to join up with some other lads in a brothel just around the corner from the ground. A few of the Chelsea lads were shagging for the whole of the game. It was £1 for a gobble and 50p for a fuck. At the time I didn't agree with prostitutes and watched a boring 0-0 draw on the telly in a dirty shit hole of a bar. I realise now I should have been having me balls sucked clean and me bollocks unloaded but you live and learn don't you? – Only joking.

After the game a few of us were drinking in a bar down on the seafront and a hundred strong mob of Turks stood outside threatening to kill us if we stepped outside for a fight. The funny, or not so funny, thing was that these cunts looked like they meant it. They were brushing their fingers across their throats in a cutting, and slicing motion and shouting insults in Turkish. We had seen a mob of Turks early on in the day down at the ground at the ticket office. A mob of them had made a circle around half a dozen of us but just sang songs and pushed into us. We ignored them and walked through them and away without any punches being thrown. This mob outside seemed to be winding themselves up and were getting more angry by the minute. Lots of them had football colours on and red painted faces. The man that ran the bar was trying to defuse the situation and ordered a couple of taxis to get us away, as they pulled up they were surrounded by the mob of angry Turks.

"Get in the taxi" I said to the others.

"Yea, get in the taxis before we cut you up" replied a Turk, almost spitting in my face as his distorted features spat out the words. I'd rather have taken them head-on and given it to them. At one stage I picked up a knife from the bar and was quite willing to mix it with the Turks but the bar owner and a few of the Chelsea lads talked me out of it.

It was my first experience of Turkey but I soon found out what the crack was. The one thing that did surprise me was the lack of Old Bill. I'd thought they'd be right on the England fans case but they were very low key. One young lad from Jersey was arrested out there for burning a Turkish flag and got 3 months inside. I'd been in trouble myself a couple of days before the game. I was in a bar with Salford and Binman in Bodrum and a coffee table got broken and the bar owner demanded that one of us pay for it.

"Fuck off" came back the reply. "The table's riddled with woodworm". Anyway, the Old Bill were called and took Binman and me away to the cells. They let us go at 6.00 a.m. the next morning after nicking a few quid off of us. To be honest we'd been well pissed and got off lightly by just being banged up for the night.

The next night I was in a bar when this half Turkish, half Canadian geezer came in the bar mouthing off how he hated the English. I ended up going outside with him and we had a bit of a scrap. When the police turned up he grassed me up and said I'd started it so I was arrested and taken to the same police station I'd been banged up in the night before. All they done was lock me up for the night, take a few more quid off me and kicked me out. The next morning I was on first name terms with the coppers and I think they were getting quite fond of me.

On the following night one of the main Chelsea lads got arrested and when he was taken down to the nick one of the coppers asked, "where's that big Gary?"

All in all we had a good week in Turkey. The weather weren't too bad and it was cheap to eat and drink, and it was an experience.

My next trip with England was out in Yugoslavia for the European qualifier game in November. We booked ten days and flew to Belgrade where we stayed for one night. It was grey and horrible and typical Iron Curtain. There was only about 500 England fans out there for the game. The only trouble was between Partisan Belgrade and Red Star Belgrade who were having rows with one another. A few of us walked around the ground for a row after the game, which England won 4-1 with goals from Beardsley, Barnes, Robson and Tony Adams, but everything passed off peacefully probably because there was that many Old Bill about.

Me, John from Sheffield, and Frankie from Nottingham, took a ten-hour train journey down to Dubrovnik, on the Adriatic coast. There was a scruffy looking fucker in our carriage who stunk. I don't know if he'd farted or shit himself but he stank so I stood up and opened the window to let the stench out, and let some fresh air in. As I sat down he stood up and closed the window and next minute he's shouted for the train guard who appeared and must have asked, in Yugoslavian, what all the commotion was. The scruffy cunt points at the window and then points at me. Everyone in the carriage is intrigued at what's going on. You could have heard a pin drop. This was theatre on the move. The guard, having heard what old scruffy bollocks has to say, turns to me and starts shouting at the top of his voice at me. "Fuck you" I reply, and sit back down and totally ignore him. When we reach Dubrovnik there's women waiting on the platform offering you accommodation. One of the places on offer works out at £1.50 each. It's up in the hills and it included a double bedroom, a single bedroom and an evening meal. Although it was a bit expensive, we just had to have it. The old town is picturesque and is surrounded by a medieval wall. It was about a 15-minute walk from the house down into the town centre. One night we ended up in this disco and a few local youths took exception to us being English. When my back was turned one of them threw a drink over me. I turned around "Come on you cunts" I said, gesturing for a fight. One of the youths could speak perfect English and tried to calm the situation down.

"It was an accident," he claimed. "My friend spilt his drink, I am sorry". Anyway they fucked off and we carried on drinking but another local told us to be careful as he had seen them drive off in two cars and that they may well ambush us. We staggered off at the end of the night and crossed the empty main square and out through a gate in the wall that led out onto the lane that took us up into the hills where our digs were. As we came out of the gate the bastards were there and they came at us. My mate legged it and I got tripped up and booted all over the place. One of them was a real big lump that put the boot in as I lay there. I staggered off into the night battered and bruised, and covered in claret. Inside my mouth was cut to ribbons and one of the Yugoslavs who spoke English pointed me in the direction of the local hospital. I found it and walked in and they saw to me straight away. I think they knew I was in a bad way and jabbed me up and stitched and bathed all my cuts and bruises. I was told to come back the next morning for another check up, and to show my passport and to pay the bill for the treatment. I didn't bother going back. They stitched me up and I stitched them up. Job done and that were it. The next day we flew back from Belgrade having learnt a valuable lesson about being English abroad.

I've lived in Nottingham for the last 15 years and moved up here with my job. I was on a Chelsea video when there was trouble out in Belgium with Brugges and that was my way in with the Forest lads because a lot of them saw me on it. I met Boatsy through my Chelsea connections. Boatsy and a few of the Forest lads had, had a bit of a row with some Chelsea mates of mine and a few from each side ended up getting nicked. Forest have always had a good firm who on their day can pull big numbers. I now know most of their lads and most of them know me as Chelsea Mark. This is the place where I live and work and Forest have a place in my heart, but Chelsea's my team and I'd never change sides. I'm Chelsea through and through and now we're Champions. Just think of the jealousy towards us. Most teams hate us now, but fuck 'em.

NAME: Mark
AGE: 36
CLUB: Chelsea

CHAPTER 7

Could This Be Our Year?

THE 87/88 season saw us go on a bit of an F.A. Cup run with victories at Halifax 4-0 in the 3rd round, a 2-1 win away at Orient in the 4th round and then a Gary Crosby goal gave us a 1-0 5th round win at Birmingham. We followed this with a 2-1 win at Highbury in the quarterfinals. Next stop was Hillsborough where we were playing Liverpool in the semi-finals.

There was a real buzz around Nottingham. There was a strong feeling that this could well be our year to lift the piece of silverware that Cloughie, had never got his hands on.

Me and half a dozen of the lads travelled up to Sheffield the night before the game and met up with me mate, John, who lived up there. We went boozing in a few pubs and ended up doing the fruit machine with a screwdriver, and banged it open. We had a few quid out of it, and were moving off to another pub when someone must have grassed us up. The Old Bill arrived, and nicked me and carted me off. They also took away me mate Gez, and we both ended up banged up for the night. They found a screwdriver on Gez and a load of pound coins on me. The cops asked me why I had so much change on me but all I replied was "no comment" and every time they asked me I would just reply "no comment". Well they were getting the right hump so they changed tactics. One copper came in and stood in front of me and in a broad Yorkshire accent said "thou knows thous done it Boatsy," and he punches me hard in the stomach and gives me a whack on the jaw.

"Come on, admit it", he said. He'd winded me but I wouldn't admit it. I later learned that he'd got my name from a big fat lad they'd pulled in after us for the same thing. They bailed us on suspicion of theft the next morning and then we went to the game, which we lost 2-1. We played the

Scousers three times on the trot in the space of about 10 days. We beat them at our place 2-1 in the League and then played Portsmouth away. Then came the semi-final game and then five days later we lost at Anfield 5-0 in the League. At the semi-final game there was only one real spot of aggro and that was when, after the game, a mob of about 200 Scousers came towards about 100 of us waiting in the park near to the ground. We casually walked towards them, threw a few punches and they were off. It was all their main boys but they didn't hang around. We scattered them everywhere before the Old Bill eventually arrived and broke it up.

A few months after I'd been arrested I was called back up to the police station in Sheffield where they dropped all the charges against me and Gez, and they even gave me back my pound coins in plastic bank bags.

I think that year we had the Cup run. The game at Birmingham, in the 5th round, was one of the best rows I've ever seen at football. It was a great one. About 50 of us got there at 11 o'clock in the morning and got a pub sorted, and another 100 got off the train from Nottingham about the same time and got settled into another pub near to New Street. 10 minutes after we arrived, the pub windows were put in as a Birmingham mob attacked the pub. We came out the pub and chased them into the city centre. Meanwhile, our lot are in their pub when a group of Birmingham's black lads come in and start throwing things around before they get chased out. So we come out of the pub we've in after hearing about the row at the train station and the two Forest mobs meet up and head towards the ground. As we walk along mobs of Birmingham are now coming at us from all sides and its running battles up side streets all the way to the ground. As we reach the ground a mob of Forest are battling with a huge mob of Birmingham, just outside the turnstiles. It's bedlam, absolute mayhem. The Old Bill had lost control and on the day, we had ten thousand fans there, with Forest taking over the entire Tilton Road end terrace and the seats in the upper tier of the Railway stand. At the end of the game, we all came out in a big mob from where we'd been standing, and as we came around behind where the rest of the Forest fans were seated, we could see Birmingham attacking them with bricks. We had a right tight mob that day and as half our mob boarded their coaches for home, we went off on manoeuvres. As we turned a corner, a mob of Birmingham appeared in front of us and ambushed us. We backed off as they launched everything imaginable at us, bricks, bottles, lumps of concrete, wood, metal piping, coins, all rained down on us. Our main man waved us forward and led the way into them. Blocking his path was a powerfully built black man who stood there in a menacing pose, fists tightly clenched at his side. Crack! Our man landed one on his jaw and he flew through the air, knocked off his feet by the sheer speed and power of the punch. Our man was famous for switching people off with one shot. We swarmed all over them and run them in all directions but the main bulk of them got chased all the way back into the city centre, where they re-grouped. It was now them one side of the road and us on the other, with the police standing in the middle separating the two mobs. We walked towards the Bullring with the two mobs just waiting to get stuck into one another. The Old Bill were really having their work cut out keeping us apart and as we entered the Bullring we were showered with more missiles. The Old Bill moved in on the throwers and that left a bit of a gap, which we took advantage of and steamed into Birmingham and ran them down the subway we were still in Birmingham city centre an hour and a half after the game. We found a pub a bit out of the way and then decided to walk back to where we'd parked our cars earlier that day. As we got back into the cars, a mob of Birmingham appeared on a flyover above us and gave us a round of applause for our efforts that day.

The next morning the Sunday papers were full of it with most headlines concentrating on the numbers of arrests and, if I remember rightly, I think there was something like 87 of them. I, for once, was not one of them.

My next England trip was the European Championship finals out in Germany. My sister was living and working out in Frankfurt at the time so all the Forest lads met up in Frankfurt. I flew out from Birmingham but a lot of the lads drove out there. All in all there was about 40 of us. We booked into different hotels and met up in a bar near the train station. On the day of the first match against the Irish, we travelled down to Stuttgart for the game. We bought tickets from a tout outside the ground and ended up in the Irish end where the dirty bastards, on finding out that we were English, started spitting on us. So much so for the lovely, friendly spirit of the Irish as always portrayed by the press. We were fronting them and offering to fight them but they shit themselves. There were only five of us but they wouldn't have it. After the game, which we lost 1-0, we had a bit of an off with some Germans near Stuttgart Station. About 50 of them came bouncing across the road towards us, throwing ball bearings along the floor to trip us up. A couple of them pulled out gas and squirted it all around. We got straight into them and run them everywhere through the shops and bars, which were close to the station. The German police inter-vened, pulled their batons out, and got a bit heavy-handed. They chased Gez around a parked car trying to clump him. It looked like a couple of kids playing kiss chase or hee! It was then back to Frankfurt where we had a bit of a scuffle with some Chinese, and then a couple of days later we headed off to Dusseldorf for the game against the Dutch.

That's the first time I met Bonzo from West Ham and him and me have been friends ever since, and we met up again recently at the launch of Bill Gardner's Book. Anyway, the papers were full of how the Dutch hooligans were turning out to show their English rivals just who was the toughest. Around the station there was mobs of English everywhere and Gez was handing out printed business cards with "The Forest Executive Crew – Do the Dutch" written on them. The Dutch firm failed to show but their fellow countrymen, dressed from head to toe in bright orange, did turn out in their thousands. Again, England was shit and we lost 3-1.

After the game we had a massive mob and when we were going over a flyover we saw below us happy Dutch fans in their orange wigs, with flags and scarves hanging out of their car windows, driving back towards the Dutch border. The English had seen enough and bombarded them with missiles. We'd sat with the Dutch inside the stadium and they never said a word to us, not even when Bryan Robson scored and we all jumped up. They never said boo to a goose. It was funny how we ended up in with them really. My two mates from Sheffield were discussing ticket prices with a couple of touts and made out they were prepared to meet their asking price but wanted to see where the tickets were in the stadium. As soon as the touts pulled them out the boys snatched them and were off.

The last game was against Russia but most people decided to go home as we were already out of the competition. I had a ticket for the match so I stayed on in Frankfurt, but the team were terrible. I did get to have a drink with me sister though so it didn't turn out too bad and oh! Yeah, I almost forgot, we lost to the Russians 3-1 with Tony Adams getting our goal.

Huddersfield in the League Cup over two legs, Watford away in the F.A. Cup, and the semi-final of the F.A. Cup against Liverpool in that terrible tragedy at Hillsborough were my next batch of nickings. The Huddersfield Town game we'd played them at home and they'd bought a coach load of lads down. We couldn't get near them though as our coppers had it sewn up that night, but fair play to Huddersfield, they did turn up and they've always had a good mob. We've never really came across them but they have a well-respected mob.

In the 2nd leg, on the day of the game about 50 of us met in a boozer on the outskirts of Nottingham and drove off to Huddersfield, which is about an hour and a half's drive away, but before we left we screwed the fruit machine and fucked off. We was in Huddersfield by 3 o'clock and as soon as we got there we had some aggro with some black lads, around near the station, who pulled knives out on us but they soon legged it back into an amusement arcade. We found a pub and by now there was about a hundred of us. We'd been in there an hour or so when their mob turned up outside so we piled out and chased them up the road. The coppers got their act together and camped outside the pub watching our every move. About 7 o'clock we decided to walk down to the ground but as we were walking along some of Huddersfield's lads were mingling in with us and giving us lip. Some idiot with them who is still in his work overalls, sidles up to me and starts gobbing off about the miners' strike and all that bollocks. I've done no more and landed one on his jaw and dropped him. A copper has seen me and I'm nicked. That was it. I was carted off and locked up. A few Forest were nicked that night and I remember them throwing us all in the same cell. They let us go about an hour after the game and it turned out that three of us who had travelled up in the same car all got nicked.

As soon as we were released we headed straight to the nearest pub, and in there was a few Huddersfield lads drinking. We never really took that much notice. They looked over at us and we glanced back at them but no bother, just a bit of an uneasy truce. We knew who they were and they knew who we were. It wasn't until a few years later at Italia 90 when one of the Huddersfield lads recognised me from the pub that night and told me that a few of the locals wanted to fill us in but he said they knew there was only a few of us so they didn't bother. After "last orders" we're driving out of Huddersfield, heading for the motorway, when the police pull us over. They tell us the registration of the car we've in matches the one Nottinghamshire Police are looking for. They then inform us that we have to go back to the police station we've just come from so that they can make more enquiries. When we walk back in the coppers behind the front desk are as baffled as us. "We've just let you go", they said. We're charged with suspicion of theft but they have no proof and we all denied it, so the charges were dropped.

About a month later I'm back up in court in Huddersfield for hitting the geezer in his Sunday best boiler suit. I receive a fine of £250, which was a lot of money in those days, and a six-month ban from football. I was banned from every football ground in the country but I wasn't that bothered. Same with the thing at Watford, it was an F.A. Cup game and was being shown live on the telly on a Sunday afternoon, but when Lee Chapman scored for us I on the spur of the moment decided to run onto the pitch to congratulate him. The Old Bill grabbed me, marched me off and locked me up in a porta cabin for a few hours. They gave me a load of bullshit about endangering players and then released me without charge.

The same season we got to the semi-final at Hillsborough where we played

Liverpool. We met up in Sheffield City in the morning and ended up in a boozer near the market. About midday, a mob of Sheffield United turned up and I was one of the first of our lads out of the door. As I stepped onto the pavement a Sheffield lad to the side of me, caught me with a sneaky sidewinder and then legged it up the road with his mates. I can't understand why they attacked the pub, as there were only about 20 of them. We then decided to catch the bus up to the ground. We walked around to the Leppings Lane end of the ground and we walked past thousands of Scousers, many of them blotto, absolutely pissed out of their skulls. Rumour had it they'd drank a couple of pubs dry of all the drink also a few of the machines had been done. About 50 of us walked through them and a couple in their whiney Scouse accents said, "hold up lads, Forest are here". I remember I had a denim shirt on and they all pointed at me as a semi-circle of them came around us. I flopped one of them and then they were all over us and I had me shirt ripped from my back as a copper grabbed me and led me away. I was taken into the ground and locked up in a porta-cabin at the back of the stand. Loads of Scousers were bought in for being drunk and disorderly and there was a little window that I could see out of. I can remember people coming out on stretchers and I was thinking, "My God it's kicked off inside the ground". Rumours soon spread that people had died in the ground. A senior copper came in and released us but wouldn't say exactly what had gone on. All he would say was that due to the circumstances of that day's events we were all being released without charge. I'd originally been charged with threatening behaviour but now I was being released with a caution.

As I came out of the ground there were still ambulances, with sirens and blue light flashing, leaving and arriving at the back of the stands. I made my way back to Sheffield station where I met up with Jimmy McGowan and a few of the Forest lads in a pub, and I still didn't know the full picture of what had gone on. A few people were ringing home and stories were coming back that 50 had died. Then someone came in the pub and said there was 100 dead. A few Scousers came in and said that those who had died were killed in a big fight, but it was all rumours. I was just glad I wasn't there to see it. It wasn't until the next day that the full extent of the tragedy unfolded I was totally, horrified no one should die at a football match no matter who you support. My thoughts and feelings go out to the people and the families of those that died. I have nothing against anybody that badly that they die at a football match. God bless you all. I can say no more.

NAME Sukkiy
AGE 36
CLUB Nottingham
Forest

My older brother first took me to Forest when I was 10 years old. He was 11 years older than me and at the time you didn't get that many Asian geezers going to football. My uncle, my dad's older brother, also went. My family originally came from the Punjab in India and are Sikhs. They came over to England in the 60s and came straight to Nottingham and Dad got a job in engineering. I grew up in Nottingham where I was born.

My first game was against Bristol City and I just loved it straight away. I loved the atmosphere. My brother was already a big Forest fan but he wasn't into the violence. When we came out we could see groups of youths fighting and I was intrigued by it all. My older brother was a bit of a black sheep and although bought up in the traditional Sikh ways, turned his back on them and got on with living a Western lifestyle. He even became a bouncer working the doors and by all accounts he was good at the job. He was a very educated person and as I got older I learnt how he had rebelled. Mind you, I used to snitch on him and go and tell me mum that I'd seen him smoking and kissing white girls. I remember him taking me to one side and him telling me that "one day you will understand," and I now know what he was on about and I do now understand. Too right I do. He was a good-looking lad who could pull the women, went to college and got brilliant grades, and he could more than handle himself.

By tradition us Sikh boys are born warriors and can be very quick tempered. He was a black belt in karate and could take your head off as quick as look at you. He took loads of shit when he was a kid growing up but he overcame it, but that was his nature. He'd never let things get him down. He'd face fire with fire. He worked the doors of The Final Solution, Tiffanys and Isabelles and was well respected by his work colleagues and the punters. I think I can remember only the one occasion when he had to resort to violence and then he nearly took this kid's head off with a roundhouse kick.

Five years ago he tragically and sadly committed suicide, and I was the one that found him hanging at his house. He'd been with his partner for 10 years and he found out that she'd been cheating on him and he took his life because he couldn't stand the pain. He loved her that much and he always said he'd give his life for her because he loved her that much, and he did. He had a son and I treat him like my own son and he's a lovely little lad who I adore and love to bits. My brother was my guiding light and spiritually he will always be with me. There isn't a day goes by when I don't think about him. I also lost my mum and sister and my other brother in a car accident. They'd just come back from holiday and were killed in a car crash near Heathrow Airport. That was so hard to deal with. Mum and dad loved each other dearly and were married for 42 years. My dad no longer wears a turban but has replaced it with an Elvis quiff. He's just had a triple by-pass operation and he's the perfect gentleman.

To me the Sikh religion has some good bits and some bad bits and I can't relate to it all. It's now the 21st century and this generation have become Westernised. Young Sikh men and women can now marry who they want. I've been out to India five times and the scenery is beautiful and the people are humble and honest. Even though some of them haven't got a lot they would die for you and I feel the same for all my mates at Forest. Hand on heart, I would die for them and they know it. They were there for me when I lost members of my family and in a funny way they all became my family.

I first met Boatsy about 10 years ago. I'd heard a lot about him before I met him. I started to hang around the lads in the early 80s and one of the main lads asked the rest of the lads. "Who's the Paki that's been hanging around us?" I used to get some right stick off of some of them. It was so racist, it was unbeliev-able. Then one of me brother's mates, Mark Anderson, who, God bless his soul has since passed away, took me under his wing. If anyone said anything Mark would tell them to leave me alone as I was with him and that seemed to do the trick, plus around this time I started to go to more games and got to know a few of the younger lads. At the time we had The Forest Executive Crew and The S.A.S. from Snenton, plus the younger lot I'd got to know called themselves The F.Y.L. (The Forest Young Lot). Basically I got stuck in with the rest of them and sometimes we lost out and sometimes we won. It was that simple. There's a few young Asian kids who now come over to Forest and who think I'm mad. I suppose they look up to me. I've got the Forest tattoos and St. George tattooed on my back. Boatsy is a very funny person, almost aloof, and if he doesn't know you he will just sit back and observe. At one time I couldn't even say hello to him and then over the course of time he got to know my face and from being a no one I became a someone. I've just been to court and got a 3-year football ban and a £500 fine, so perhaps I really am a someone now?

Hampon Park,
with England.

Italy 1990, World
Cup. With Dale
and a few of the
boys.

Our mob, Sheffield
United, home.

Above: On the way to Poznan, Brandenburg Gate, Berlin. Ready for battle!

Left: New York. On a trip with the ex-wife.

Below: Niagra Falls.

On the Pitch at the City ground.

Sheffield United, early nineties, on Maid Marion Way..

Peter bro away, where were U.

Day out in London.

Maid Marion Way, Robin Hood's men.

Down Mexico way with Shaun (told him years ago to get rid of that thing above the lip).

Me and my best mate Dave, one of Forest's finest.

Sanish hospitality, Santander 1992.

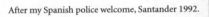

After my Spanish police welcome, Santander 1992.

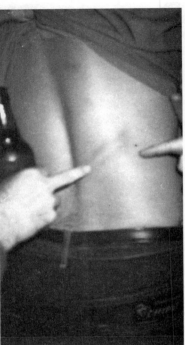

Santander, with England.

Turkey, away. Where
Europe meets Asia.

Amsterdam.

Blue Mosque, Istanbul.

Me and Nicky, top Forest
boy, who's just done Andy
Nichols latest book, *A-Z of
Football Firms*.

CHAPTER 8

The Naughty Nineties

Part 1

WE WERE playing Manchester United in the 3rd round of the F.A. Cup at our place. Alex Ferguson, the United Manager, was under a bit of pressure to turn United into a trophy winning side and the media were giving him a bit of a hard time.

We met early, but to tell you the truth we had a bit of a disappointing turn out and we bumped into the United firm just before Trent Bridge. 20 or 30 of us had come along London Road and we ran straight into them. I think the game was live on Sunday T.V. It was just about to go off with both mobs strolling towards one another, arms outstretched in battle pose, when I spot my United mate in amongst them. He sees me and shouts and waves at me. I shout back and wave at him and the Old Bill come across the road and nick me. The copper tells me he's seen my aggressive behaviour and he's arresting me for threatening behaviour. I'm handcuffed and thrown into the police van that he's just screeched to a halt in. So in fact, he'd seen fuck all. I'm taken to the ground and put in the police cells underneath the Executive Stand and after the game; I'm released and charged with a Section 5. The desk sergeant on duty is the same copper I used to play cricket with years before and he shook his head and smiled, and let out a sarcastic laugh.

"I told you Gary, you should have stuck to a more gentlemanly game like cricket. Take a look at yourself Gary", he went on, "Whatever has happened to you?"

A couple of weeks later I was up in front of the magistrate for this case of wrongful arrest, and received a conditional discharge. I was going to ask my mate from Manchester to go as a witness for me but decided against it. The way I saw it, it would only prolong things, drag things out and involve other people. Anyway, it turned out not too bad in the end. The conditional discharge meant that I had to keep out of trouble for the next 6 months and if I did it would be wiped off my record.

At the game United won 1-0 with a Mark Robbins goal, and Alex Ferguson was at last smiling. If Forest had won that cup game then I'm sure United would never have gone on to win all them trophies. But as they say the rest is history.

For the Italia 90 tournament me and me mate, Scriv, got an Inter-rail card each, which enabled us to travel around Europe by train on the cheap. The first game for England in the tournament was against Ireland in Cagliari, which finished in a 1-1 draw with Gary Lineker getting the goal for England, but we didn't bother with that one. The next game was five days later against Holland and again, out in Sardinia. We got as far as Boulogne and watched the game on T.V. in a little French bar. It was a dour game, which finished 0-0. The only good thing was that this trip was being sponsored courtesy of a dodgy Visa card that one of the Forest lads had acquired, so all the meals and most of our bar bills and our shopping in the chic French boutiques were paid for by the generous Mr. X. I sort of, remember getting paralytic drunk in a bar full of Frenchmen with no-one, surprise surprise, but only us, cheering on the English team. Just before the end Stuart Pearce scored for England but we were that pissed and celebrating the goal so wildly that we didn't see the referee disallow it. Even the next morning we were still thinking that we'd won 1-0. The evils of drink eh?

Our next stop was Paris where we got friendly with some American girls on the train down to Toulon. We nicknamed the train The Sex Express for obvious reasons. We shared some wine and booze with them and things just progressed from there. I was now a single fella after my long-time girl-friend, Clare, had left me. We were living together but one day she just came home and decided she'd had enough of me and went off back to her mum's. She was just a bit young and I was just a bit daft, but there you go. We remained mates. These yanks weren't the greatest birds in the world but when you want to unload your bollocks, who gives a fuck. It's a man's thing.

After our nibble on the train, we arrived relieved in more ways then one in Toulon, and we were going to go on from there to Sardinia to catch, the next game, against Egypt. We'd heard all the talk about if you were English and you misbehaved in Sardinia then you're going to get nicked. The police were using a zero tolerance policy so we thought "fuck it". It was £80 one way on a ferry so we decided to have a few nights out on the old "pay as you go" card. We had a quality night in Cannes, which was bang on, and we then stopped at St. Raphael for the night before crossing the border into Italy. We watched the Egypt game on T.V. in a bar in some holiday resort and I remember as we arrived I was expecting the police, the army, and customs to be waiting for this English invasion. We didn't even have to show our passports. We watched the Scotland v Brazil game prior to our game. England ended up winning 1-0 with a Mark Wright header, so we were through to the next stage.

There was some Glasgow Rangers' fans stopping in our hotel, even though they'd just lost to Brazil they were bang on and a good crack and we ended up having a right good session with them. We were just praying we'd beat the Egyptians. England had played three times now and we'd not seen a single game live. Now there was a five-day gap before we played Belgium in the second round, down in Bologna, so we decided to jump on a train and spend the weekend with my sister and give the old card a bit of a bashing in Frankfurt. We caught the night train and settled down to a good night's kip. Them Europeans have got it sussed when it comes to train journeys. Most of the seats on their trains pull out into beds. We met up with me sister in Germany, had a few free meals courtesy of Mr Wong, and after the weekend we caught the night train down to Bologna.

The night before we arrived back in Italy, English fans had rioted in the seaside resort of Rimini. We arrived at 10 o'clock at Bologna Central Station and there was Italian riot police everywhere. It was like Fort Knox after what had happened in Rimini the previous night and they were checking every fucker. You couldn't move for Italian Old Bill. There was a two-day booze ban on before the game but we managed to sneak off and find a little back street bar where we quenched our thirsts. I even got a ticket for the game. I'd joined the England Travel Club and gave me grandma's address and got a six month temporary membership, but when they checked me out later I was told that I was a known hooligan and was kicked out, no questions or explanations or counselling. I was just thrown out and that was that.

My ticket was for behind the goal with the bulk of the England fans, it was at the end where David Platt scored the winner. There was a bit of minor trouble at half time but the heavy-handed Italian police soon squashed it with tear gas and a few cracked English skulls.

After the game we caught a night train down to Rome, which was packed with English fans, and it was standing room only as there wasn't a single spare seat. There was thousands of English fans on board all the trains heading for Rome. From Rome we headed to the holiday resort of Sorrento, which is about 45 minutes from Naples, and where England's next game against Cameroon was being held.

Forest had a good mob of about 40 top lads in the resort and we had 5 days just lazing in the sun. I bumped into Dennis, one of Derby's main faces, in the street one day when I was out doing a bit of shopping. He had a bit of panic in his voice as he asked me if I could sort it out so that there'd be no problems between Forest and Derby.

"We don't want trouble", he said. "After all, we're all here on England Duty". I just laughed and told him that the best thing to do was to keep out of our way and there'd be no problems and that's what they did. I never saw him or any of them again. They must have listened to my advice and kept a low one. But then again, Dennis 'as always been a sensible and decent fella and someone who, besides the team he supports, I would always have a beer with. He's a nice lad and someone I've got time for.

At the game Cameroon had about 200 fans there but for atmosphere I don't think I've been at a better England game. It was just incredible. The noise made the hair on the back of my neck stand up. It made you proud to be English. We won the game 3-2 and what an exciting game. There was no trouble but for pure excitement, you couldn't beat it. We were 2-1 down with about 10 minutes to go when England won a penalty after Lineker was chopped down. He picked himself up to coolly stick the penalty away to make it 2-2. In extra time Lineker again slotted home from the spot to seal a 3-2 England win.

I'd now been away from work at Boots for nearly two weeks. There was no way I was going to miss the semi-final game against the Germans in Turin, so I got my grandma to phone up work and tell them that I'd just got back from Italy and that I had a terrible dose of diarrhoea. That was me covered.

So it was another train journey north, back up to Turin. A lot of the English lads were now running out of money and holiday leave so just a few of us Forest lads got a hotel opposite the train station. With us was Steve, an Arsenal fan, who had moved up to Nottingham. He'd met a bird out in Sardinia while out there for the first couple of England games and is still with her to this day, and now lives out in Italy. Who said holiday romances never last? Him and me shared a big splif outside the hotel the night before our game. Fucking hell it blew my socks off and I was stoned out of my head after just a couple of draws on it. I was well and truly fucked. I remember that night through a smoky haze and that same night Argentina beat Italy to send the Italians out. Roaming the streets was a mob of

Juventus Ultras, about 300 handed, looking for the English. As we stood puffing and without a care in the world, they spotted us but hey man, who gave a fuck? It was love and peace and let's all be brothers, well it was until a car screeched to a halt in between them and us, and out jumped these blokes who turned out to be plain-clothes coppers, and they told us to get back into the hotel. Apparently, the Italians were looking for revenge for the Heysel Stadium disaster. I took my belt off and wrapped it around my knuckles in preparation of a row but it seemed to just fizzle out.

The next morning there was another alcohol ban on so to beat it we went off to the local supermarket early, bought a load of cans and bottles, filled up the bath in our room with cold water, and chilled the beer in the icy depths. Clever or what?

About midday a mob of 200 Germans came off the train and out into the street. It was kicking off and we steamed out of the hotel and into them. It was like fighting 2oo Rudi Voller clones with their permed hair, moustaches and denim dungarees. They all looked like German porn stars coming down the road at us. It lasted, all of 30 seconds a bit like a German porn star, before we legged them everywhere. They were two bob. The fight moved further up the road to a park. We all got on there and Denton, from Arsenal, cracked this Kraut on the jaw with a peach of a punch and sparked him straight out. The German had sunglasses or goggles on and they went flying as he fell to earth. I think the youth was coming for me and Denton just clocked him. That's the first time that I'd seen him for a few years. He'd been up to Forest a few times with the Gooners and he'd filled out a bit. We got tickets for the game and were seated on the halfway line but was surrounded by Krauts. There was only three of us together and when the national anthems came on the Germans around us stood up and were whistling and booing our national anthem. We stood up and stared at them and all their arses dropped as silence fell around us. The game ended with us going out on penalties and the English fans didn't take defeat too well. Our main man decked the first German he saw and I was ripping their flags down as we left the ground, we whacked every German that dared get in our way. They were shitting themselves. We got back into the centre on a train and we bumped into Gary, me mate from Manchester, and 20 of his mates.

"They look a bit handy," said our main man, giving the once over.

"Fucking hell," said Gary "Your main lad looks a bit tasty".

I think it's called mutual respect. I'd known Gary for years and how we met was most bizarre. Just before I'd started my job at Boots me Dad sent me off to work with an Irish relative of his up in Farmworth, which is near Bolton. We were doing demolition work at Kersley Power Station and he was a typical Paddy. He was dressed in a suit jacket, shirt and tie, and steel toe capped boots, and had a bright red face. I lived in a porta cabin on site so when everyone else fucked off home I had to play guard dog. I was bored one Thursday night and ventured down to the local pub. In there was Gary and a few of his pals and we got talking, which soon turned into football talk, and he sort of took me under his wing, and we've been good mates ever since. I was earning good money in them days but it was hard work. However, I learned a valuable lesson and that was how not to dress like me Irish Uncle!

England's final game was a third place play-off in Bari against Italy where we lost 2-1.

Back home I was called into the office at Boots and they basically said that they knew I was pulling a fast one and didn't believe that I'd been sick, but due to the law they would still pay me. Still, I stayed there for another year and kept me nose clean.

I've been going to Forest for just over 3 years. The first game I ever went to was Forest at home in a friendly against the Indian national side. I went with my cousin and a few mates from Beeston. When we got to the ground there were thousands of Indians at the game, but no trouble. Afterwards, on the train home, we had a bit of trouble with some Indians. We were singing our songs and they were singing theirs, and as we got up to get off at our stop, one of their lads blocked our way and tried to stop us. He put his foot up to stop us getting past, and as he stood up my cousin nutted him and there was a big scrap. There was 10 of us and 6 of them, and a while after we all got dawn raided. After that us young lot got together and were very active. We called ourselves The Forest Nasty Squad and we even had calling cards made up. At the height of our exploits, we numbered around 40 lads, maybe 50 at times.

NAME: Fred
AGE: 22
CLUB: Nottingham Forest

A couple of the young lot knew Boatsy because they worked with him. At times we'd try to impress his lot by being in the frontline when it kicked off, and just tried to show that if it went off, we were game. Some of the older lads used to give us a bit of stick but I think we've done our bit. Every club as got a youth mob now and it seems to be getting bigger. I'd heard all our older lads' names when I was still at school and some when I came on the scene. It was like I had to prove myself.

We had a battle with the Burnley youth mob in Blackpool and a few lads had to go to court over that. The last few seasons things were going well as we had our own web site and were in touch with all the youth firms from around the country. We kept ourselves separate from our older lot and we had our own identity. We'd organise it that any rows were strictly youth on youth and we'd try to keep it that way, but sometimes we'd bump into other teams' main lads and we'd give them a good bash. But banning orders have played a big part in killing it altogether and I think the scene is nearly dead. We tried to breathe some life back into it but I think we just caught the tail end of it. Maybe it could well get a third wind and maybe, for old times sake, the youth and the old lot will turn out for that one big game. Who knows? It may well happen. I've been in court 4 times and just recently I received a banning order so that's me out of the game. No more dawn raids for me.

A COUPLE OF mates from Sheffield and five of us from Nottingham, flew to Berlin for a few days and then travelled down into Poland for the European Championship qualifier in Poznan. We had a bit of a spend-up and a few free meals and drinks on a dodgy card. We'd got cheap flights out of one of the papers and it was a "pay for one, get one free" type deal.

Part 2

It was freezing cold when we arrived in Poznan after a 4 hour train journey, and what a culture shock it was. It was a cold, grey, faceless place and I remember one of the lads had some funny £10 notes, which were cashed up into the local currency. We stuck a £10 note behind the bar, which lasted all day. We got a taxi to the ground and as we stepped from the taxi it was going off all around us. "Fucking hell", I remember thinking, "this is brilliant", and I've got to give it to the Poles, they were as game as fuck. The game ended in a 1-1 draw with Lineker getting on the score sheet.

After the game we were kept in for half an hour and a few of the Chelsea lads were getting a bit bored so they decided to get onto the pitch. Behind one goal there was no stand and a few of the Chelsea boys found a petrol lawn mower, got it started, and drove it onto the pitch and drove it around the goal posts. They then took penalties with an imaginary ball as the rest of the English hordes cheered them on. The Polish Old Bill took it all good heartedly and even they thought it was as funny as fuck. After the game, we never saw any Polish fans so we caught a cab back to the bar, which we'd been in before the game. I got chatting to a couple of Polish girls who were out with their dad, and we ended up sharing a few bottles of wine together. I swear I still had change from the original tenner I'd put behind the bar. The funny thing was it was a wrong 'un anyway. I bet that bar owner was well pleased when he went to the bank to cash it.

Norwich City in the 6th round of the F.A. Cup was my next spot of bother. Roy Keane scored in a 1-0 win. We'd played Southampton in the previous round and after drawing 1-1 at The Dell; we beat them 3-1 at the City ground. The game at The Dell was on a Monday night and it was live on Sky. Nigel Clough equalised with 10 minutes to go and I remember taking two days off work to take in the game. The game at Norwich saw all our boys get down there early and in no time at all we had a 200 strong mob and it wasn't long before we got on the rob and the fruit machines got done over. We made a nice few quid that day from the pubs in the town centre. All their boys were in a pub called something like The Warriors. Anyway, we were in another pub just around the corner from them. Behind the pub we were in was a maze of alleyways and lanes with shoe shops and craft shops. Next minute the shout went up that Norwich were here. We all piled out and they were as game as fuck. I remember grabbing some shoes off a shoe display and hitting some cunt over the head with them. I couldn't believe it. They were well up for it and it went toe-to-toe for a good minute and was a proper row. Half of our lot were still drinking in the pub and hadn't a clue what was going on outside. The Old Bill arrived and separated the two mobs and we were pushed back into the pub, and half an hour before the game we were allowed to leave under police escort. We were led down to the ground and once inside we found our seats, which were all down the side. Just before the end of the game I could see one of our coppers from Nottingham talking to a Norwich copper who called me over. I took no notice as he pointed in my direction with a finger motion to come out of the crowds and speak to him.

"Come here", he mouthed. Eventually I got up and squeezed my way along the row of bodies.

"Right you, you're under arrest", he said.

"What for?" I replied.

"Suspicion of theft", he says.

I was taken to Norwich police station and all in all they'd arrested five of us for the same offence. They kept us until ten o'clock that night and then they released us without charge. It was just an excuse to get us off the streets. They said it was for prevention. One of the lads phoned The Fountain pub in Nottingham and one of our lads drove down to pick us up and run us home. For him it was a six-hour round trip but then what are mates for?

The semi-final was against West Ham, who we beat 4-0. Most people remember that game for the sending off, of West Ham's Tony Gale, which some might say was a bit harsh. On the day West Ham had a massive mob strolling about outside Villa Park before and after the game. I went with a girlfriend, mainly to keep out of bother, but all our lads were there but for some reason we just didn't get it together that day. It's funny how these things pan out. On some occasions you can pull a huge mob out of nothing, and at other times everyone's split up and so and so and his boys are in one pub and there's another 100 drinking in another boozer, and somehow or other you don't get to meet up and get it together. I did hear that West Ham's mob tried to steam the Forest turnstiles, but they really had no one to fight. As I say, we were in dribs and drabs and it seemed we were there that day purely to enjoy the day out and the football.

In the Final we played Spurs. I was a season ticket holder that season so my Cup Final ticket cost me £18. A bloke at work kept on and on badgering, for me to sell my ticket to him and in the end we agreed a price and he handed over £200. I was going down to London on the Friday night before the game so that £200 would pay for my weekend.

On the morning of the game we was in The Dolphin pub, just off the Euston Road, by 9 o'clock and even that early we had a good set of lads out. We'd turn up there every year when we played in a Final at Wembley. It was our second home and we got to know the Governor of the pub quite well and were well-behaved and good spenders so he didn't mind letting us in early. We didn't see a Tottenham fan until we got off the tube and were walking down Wembley Way. It was Forest fans everywhere you looked, a sea of red and white. I fancied us to win it that year and so did a lot of Forest fans. I made myself busy trying to buy a cheap or face-value ticket, and began to wonder if I'd done the right thing in selling my ticket. I had a bit of doubt now I was there and could hear and see the atmosphere. Our main copper was stood further up on the top of Wembley Way filming us with his video camera. There was the odd scuffle and a bit of verbal with the odd Spurs fan, but nothing too serious. I was standing chatting to a mate when this big, white bloke comes walking over and stands next to me. I thought he was selling tickets the way he looked around to see if anyone was watching or listening. This was more James Bond than Match of the Day, and then he spoke out of the corner of his mouth. Perhaps he'd watched too much of 'Man From Uncle' as a kid, but I gave him ten out of ten for suspense. He kept me hooked for all of ten seconds and the effect was first rate. All he needed was a Trilby hat pulled down to the tip of his nose and a trench Mac with the collar turned up.

"Boatsy" he said, not looking at me but having a quick look around "Get your boys together", he growled in a gruff, cockney accent, "And we'll take a walk up the road and we'll have it with ya".

"Yea righto mate, no problem", I replied and then I thought hold up he just said my name. How the fuck did he know my name? He must have asked one of our lot who our main boy was and some cunt must have pointed at me and told him to see "Boatsy". I was shocked and didn't have a clue who this big lump was, but he was massive. All the coppers were watching as I rounded up our lads and we could see this Spurs mob now hanging about and giving us the eye. We had a good 50 of us without tickets who were sticking together. We'd planned that once the game had kicked off we'd go back to Kilburn and watch it in 'The Roman Way' on the telly.

We walked off and about 40 of this Spurs lot followed, and straight away I noticed they had a lot of young ones with them. The Old Bill followed in a van, but as we got up near the tube station they had for some reason best known to them, had dwindled off and had given up the chase. We turned a corner and suddenly Tottenham appeared in front of us. They lobbed empty milk bottles at us and then legged it. Neanderthal Man was nowhere to be seen as we chased them up the road. The Old Bill re-appeared and screeched to a halt in a van and herded us onto the tube. Me mate Darryl said after the game, which we lost yet again in an F.A. Cup final, that Tottenham had a massive firm afterwards and they were looking for us. We were so disappointed with that 2-1 defeat that most of us just went back to Kings Cross straight after the game, and caught the first train back to Nottingham. I for one was gutted. So near, yet so far still we had won the greatest prize in Europe, not once but twice, but the F.A. Cup was one of them competitions where, it seemed, we could never quite get over that final hurdle and get our hands on that famous piece of silverware.

T HE EUROPEAN Championship finals in Sweden in '92 just didn't appeal to me. I'd been there for a World Cup qualifier in '89. Two carloads of us from Nottingham caught the boat from Harwich to Hamburg, where we did all the sex shows, meals and drinks on a dodgy credit card. It was total freebies. We hired cars and drove up to the German ferry port of Kiel. From there it was a boat trip across to Malmo in Sweden. That game ended 0-0 and in '89 a bottle of beer was £5, so for the Euros in '92 I thought I'd just give it a miss. It was just too expensive for hotels and to eat and drink out, even on someone else's credit card. However, when we went 1-0 up with a goal from Platt, I rung around a few of the lads at half-time and we all said that if we won that game we would all meet down at the travel agents first thing in the morning to book a trip out to Sweden. In the second half Sweden came out and attacked England and changed their formation. It ended with the Swedes winning 2-1 and England out of the tournament, and on their way home us lot cancelled our proposed trip and stayed at home

Derby away, around this time, was another non-event in terms of not seeing or bumping into their tin-pot mob. We never saw anything of them before the game so afterwards we decided to mob up and go looking for them in their city centre. The Old Bill quickly cottoned on to what we were up to and herded us into a nearby park where we were all lined up and had our names and addresses taken. The head Old Bill was getting right pissed off and ordered his colleagues to arrest the ringleaders. They picked eight of us out and carted us off to Derby police station where they kept us until 9 o'clock at night on a prevention of the breach of the peace, and then let us go without charge. We were allowed back out onto the streets on our own, free to roam. We could quite easily have gone off and looked for Derby's firm but that wasn't a wise idea because there was only eight of us and the rest of our lot were back in Nottingham.

Part 3

I'd recently sold my house, which had doubled in price, so I hadn't really had a steady job for a couple of years as I was living on the money from my house sale. I'd been out to see my sister in America just after I'd left the job at Boots. I'd been at Boots for near on five years and left to go out to the States for 6 months. My sister was living in Tucson, Arizona, where she had a house on the edge of the desert. It had a swimming pool and an outdoor Jacuzzi. She was a student and had married an American service man who she had met while living and working in Germany. I had a two-week holiday in L.A. with a few of the lads, and after that, I caught the Greyhound bus down to Phoenix and then on to Arizona. It's only about 50 miles from the Mexican border and the weather is spot on all the year round. The Americans loved my accent and it was a great crack, and I was just getting used to the idea of maybe stopping for good when, after five weeks, I fell out with me sister. I got into a strop one day and on the spur of the moment flew off home. It was a silly row but it wasn't long before we made up and I was back out there. Almost immediately I met an American girl called Heather who was a waitress in the bar we were in. I happened to mention to my brother-in-law that the waitress was a bit of all right and he got her phone number for me. I asked her out and we ended up spending six weeks together. She was at university during the day and waitressing of a night, but it didn't last. It wasn't long before I was back in Nottingham, ducking and diving, and earning a few quid here and there.

Around this time I was consciously trying to keep out of trouble and away from football because I'd been to see my solicitor and was suing the police in Nottingham for these prevention arrests, which had happened in Norwich and Derby. It seemed I had a good case but it dragged on for nearly two years. I'd even got, legal aid so I knew I had a good case. I knew that if the case went in my favour I was due to get a few quid, but then just before it went to trial, like an idiot, I got myself nicked down in Birmingham. I was gutted as the nice few quid I was going to get, had gone out of the window. I'd even changed my group of friends and mixed with different people. I'd even met my future wife in a bar in town and everything was looking rosy and good.

The last bit of bother I'd really been in at club level was against Man United in the '92 League Cup final in April at Wembley. A few weeks before the game with United, Forest had played down in London against Wimbledon and United were playing some one else in London on the same day. A few of our lads were in a pub near Kings Cross after our game and one of them had a metal Forest pin badge on. A few United lads came in and wanted to kick it off with our lads but one of United's main lads, who's a mate of mine from a long way back, stepped in and stopped it. He told our lads to tell me to get my lads together and to come to Kilburn High Street at midday on the day of the game at Wembley. As soon as I got the message, I told everybody and went down the night before the game.

There was trouble all over the West End that night and the Forest lads more than held their own. The mob I was with caught hold of a few mancs around Covent Garden who took a bit of slap.

The morning of the game we were in The Dolphin pub at Kings Cross, nice and early. We had a little B and B we were stopping in just around the corner from the pub. It was a Sunday morning and the streets of London were near on deserted with no workers or shoppers, just the odd commuter. A lot, of the older lads were not particularly bothered about the arranged row and were more content to have a few pints and take in the day. Us younger lot were more keen and hungry and were right up for it.

As arranged, at bang on midday, a hundred strong mob of us got off the train at Kilburn. As we came out of the station, we chased a small group of scally Manc scouts up the road. As we walked in the direction where they'd just run, pub after pub of geezers emptied out onto the street. There was fucking hundreds of them. There must have been 500 of them at least and they threw everything they had at us, beer cans, full and empty, bottles, and glasses. It was like Agincourt, but sponsored by a brewery, as missiles rained down on us from the air, we stood solid and took it, but as soon as the toe-to-toe fighting started, we just got swamped and overran. There were just too many of them. Half of us got legged into a little Irish pub near the Viaduct, about 30 of us had it with a similar number of them up a side street, and our lad, Pele, had a one on one with their top half-caste Paki lad in the middle of the street. I took some potatoes off a fruit and veg display from a corner shop and was lobbing all sorts at them. The pub where some of our lads took refuge was smashed to smithereens.

While all this was going on some local resident had a hand-held video camera out of his flat window and was filming it. A few months after the event it was shown on national T.V. and the footage showed us being legged up the road, and I have to admit it that United destroyed us that day. No excuses. The ones I was with fucked off over to Wembley licking our wounds but when we got inside the stadium it was going off big time in our end. There was two thousand United fans in with us in our seats and at half time it was going mental with scrapping going on all over the place. How did united fans get hold of so many tickets nobody knows? Well, to put it another way, nobody has admitted to knowing how they got hold of so many tickets for our end. The whole event stunk with lots of finger

With my mates Chris and Jeff from The Dog's Bollocks bar Thailand – Top Boys.

Enough said.

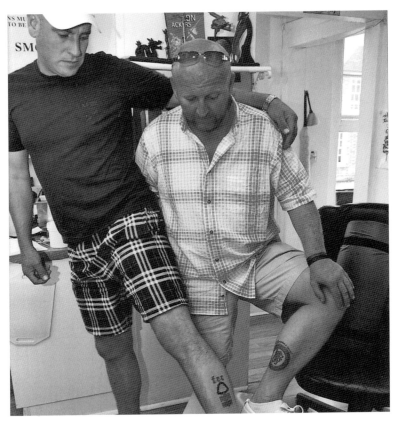

Mine's better than your's.

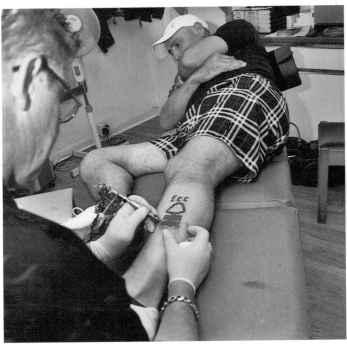

Bill in action with me suffering.

With Bill Middleton the top tattooist in the country at his Hornet Tattoo Studio in Chichester.

West Ham away in Cup, Blind Beggar,
Whitechapel, with Dale and Butler.

Real Madrid duguout. I came on for second half.

Top: My mate from school, Ashley, in France 1998.

Centre: Forest and Mansfield mob, Field Mill against the Dingels Chesterfield. Over 400 out that day.

Right: Atlantic Bar, Pattaya – two gud mates.

On tour with MK in Barcelona.

Me, Cass and Trev one of Forest's finest.

Top Boys book do in Nottingham with Cass (top bloke).

With West Ham legend Bill Garner after his book launch – A total Gentleman.

With Andy Nicholls (Everton) at Bill Garner's book launch, West Ham.

pointing and Chinese whispers and many people coming under suspicion, some within the club. We lost that final 1-0 and to many Forest fans, that defeat signalled the Club's decline.

The following season we were relegated to the old Second Division and that was the end of the Brian Clough era. He resigned at the end of that season and had stated that even if we had of stayed up he would have still left the Club.

Our last home game of the season saw us lose 2-0 to Sheffield United. After the game, I went out for a meal with my fiancé and while we were out we heard reports that parts of the city centre were being smashed up with shop windows being smashed and looted and cars being overturned and set on fire. Everyone had turned out to cause mayhem, everyone that is except me.

The last game saw us playing at Ipswich and we took over the ground and the town. One thing Cloughie did in his time, as manager was to put Forest, as a small club, on the map of world football.

Anyway, back to me losing a fortune due to my nicking at Birmingham. All the lads were going down to Birmingham for a League game so I decided to tag along for the crack. We hadn't played them for a few years since our battles down there in the F.A. Cup. There was a 100 strong mob of us in a boozer before the game when in walks one of their black lads. He told us that they had a few lads waiting for us in a pub down the road Mr. Qs, or something like that it was called. Right our lot are thinking, it's game on. We all piled out of the pub and crossed over the dual carriageway and past New Street Station, but the Old Bill who had been watching us from a distance since we had arrived had clocked us leaving the pub and followed along behind us. As we reached the pub they told us they were in a few of them came out and tried to calm it down.

"There's not enough of us here yet," one of them claimed, and a few of our lot stopped and were listening to what these blokes had to say I thought, "Fuck it," and took a swing at one of them and they backed off. The coppers came steaming in and we disappeared into a pub down a side street. The coppers burst into the pub after us, and grabbed hold of me. I'm taken outside and bundled into a police van.

A few weeks later I'm up in court and have thirty witness statements to testify that I'd not been involved in any trouble. Six of them even turned up in court to give evidence on my behalf. But I was still found guilty, even though I had a top London barrister representing me in a magistrate's court. I received 80 hours community service, a couple of hundred pound fine and banned from football for a year. That was the end of my case for compensation for my arrests for Prevention. I'd been a right idiot.

Around this time I also lost a good friend of mine, Gez. I met him through my ex-girlfriend, Claire, and although he was a Forest fan, he was more into the England scene. He was only a short bloke, about 5ft 4", but fairly stocky and looked half Italian, and he was as funny as fuck and he'd have you in stitches. He was always ducking and diving and knew how to earn a few quid. He sadly committed suicide at the age of 27 and people who knew him well couldn't believe it. He was a top, top fella who is sadly missed by us all and he is still talked about to this day. Gez The Legend lives on. God bless ya son.

Swedish police
make us feel
welcome back in
Europe.

Our mob in
London

Outside Nottingham station after a game.

Ugly mug.

France 1998. Spot of sight-
seeing where van Gogh
done a lot of his work.

In Toulouse Square before
Romania game.

With Mansfield boys, France 1998. In Lille before Colombia game.

Toulose 1998.

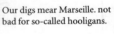

Our digs mear Marseille. not bad for so-called hooligans.

With my mate from
Newcastle, Paul Peet (top
boy), Skeeny and Shaun.

In Prague with Eddie from Newcastle and
young Adam.

Another hiding for Scouse
Dave, after a rumble with a
Prague doorman.

Prague, stag do.

Mansfield's finest in Athens 2001 for the World Cup game. Dave Butler, Ryan, and Parma taking centre stage as usual.

Part 4

ALTHOUGH I'D kept out of trouble for a few years following Forest I'd still been to the odd England game. I flew out for a World Cup qualifier in Turkey. Three of us had a weekend in Istanbul, and then we had a 12 hour, boat trip along the Bosphrus river to some town in the middle of nowhere and from there we had a 10 hour train journey to Izmir. I think that whole trip cost something like £5 I can't really remember a lot about it as I was as pissed as a fart. In the ground, the Turks threw everything they could lay their hands on at us. You had to have pull your coat over your head and some people even used their England flags to protect themselves from the bottles, some of them were filled with piss, plus you had to deal with the rocks, the cans and the coins. It was a nightmare and it went on all through the game.

Afterwards about 30 of us managed to sneak away for a row with the Turks. We were right up for it after what we'd suffered at the hands of them dirty bastard fans. We could see a mob of them standing on a street corner and we headed towards them. Before we could kick it off the Old Bill spotted us and put us on a police bus. The rest of the England fans were held back inside the ground, and then led outside and then put on coaches to take them away from the stadium. As they got down the road, they were ambushed by thousands of Turks who bricked every window in the coaches they were travelling in. We were a bit luckier as the Turkish police sailed straight past their mob with us hidden in the back of their vans. We all agreed, it was a good job we didn't get any further up the road when we went looking for a row. We were dropped off at various hotels in Izmir and were told to keep out of the way and out of trouble. A few Mansfield lads got caught doing fake money and got four and five months in a Turkish jail. I can remember sitting outside a bar one day when I saw a group of the Mansfield lads strolling past. With them was Palmer with his sunglasses on his head, posing. He later claimed in a best selling book that he was Britain's best looking football hooligan, and since that appeared he has become a gay icon with a big homosexual following. Only joking Johnathan.

Another game was against Holland in Rotterdam. England fans were just going mad so the Dutch police blocked the road off and arrested, what must have been, 500 fans. We were put in an army camp with no drink or food. We were not even allowed to use the toilets. Lots of people with tickets for the match were getting restless as kick-off time approached. A few lads got talking to a few of the guards and distracted their attention as the rest of us pulled a fence down and got out onto some marshland and legged it off into the darkness. This was the real Great Escape! I found a road and followed it until I came to a tram stop. From there, I managed to catch a tram back into the city centre and found a bar, which was showing the game on T.V. I got some strange looks from other drinkers as my bottom half was covered in dirt and thick mud. I heard later that the Old Bill had searched for us with dogs and that a helicopter had been scrambled and was flying low with search lights scanning the surrounding fields.

Poland in Katowice was nearly a disaster before we'd even got there. Me and me mate were driving down to Heathrow to catch our flight when I realised I'd forgotten my passport so we had to come off the motorway at Milton Keynes and go back to Nottingham to pick it up off of the kitchen table, which is where I'd left it. When we eventually arrived at the airport, we'd missed our flight by an hour but the check-in girls booked us onto the first available flight the following morning. As we had some time on our hands we had a night out on the town in London.

When we arrived in Berlin, we didn't have enough time to travel onto Poland for the game so we spent the night out in Germany on the piss. I even had to phone up home to get the score of the game, which ended in a 1-1 draw with Ian Wright scoring for England. I heard later that the Poles were well up for it and when they couldn't get near any England fans to fight they started to fight amongst themselves. Apparently, loads of them were skinheads with green and blue flight jackets, army greens and high legged Dr. Martens up near to their knees. They were also great big lumps who looked like they were either miners or ship builders. They do breed them big in Eastern Europe. Perhaps it's all that cabbage soup.

Spain in Santander was also another trip that nearly all went wrong even before we'd left. We drove down to Plymouth on the Sunday to catch the Monday morning ferry across to Bilbao in Northern Spain. When we went to board there was police there checking peoples passports. Rumours soon spread amongst the queue that the police were on the look out for English football hooligans trying to make the trip. When our turn arrived they looked at us, looked at the passports mumbled something and then went off with them, returning ten minutes later.

"Why are you going to Spain?" asked the copper, still studying my passport closely.

"My mate works on a campsite out there so I'm visiting him for a few days", I replied.

"So you're not going out for the football then?"

"No".

"Only we've got you on our list of known hooligans and so you're not being allowed to travel on this ferry".

What could I say to that? We'd paid £150 each and we weren't going anywhere. I protested about how much I'd paid for this trip and how we'd driven all the way down from Nottingham, but all they would say was "you're not getting on this ferry". After a while they gave us a full refund in cash. We both said "fuck the Old Bill, we can't let them beat us that easy", so we went into Plymouth town centre, found a travel agent and booked a flight from Heathrow for the next day. We drove back up to London, had the night out on the town and flew out the next day, which was the Tuesday, and the game was on the Wednesday. When we arrived in Spain, we caught a bus from Bilboa airport to Santander. We flew with Iberia for £175 but we had to stay a Saturday night, which meant we had to fly back on the Sunday. That was all part of the cheap rate ticket price.

When we got to the game there was only about 300 England fans in the stadium. I noticed me mate Jock, who I knew from previous England trips. I had a bit of a chat with him when I noticed the Spanish Old Bill weren't allowing the England fans to tie their St. George flags and union jacks to the perimeter fence. Apparently, word on the street was as this game was live on telly right across Europe then the Spanish police were going to show the Spanish people that they knew how to deal with English hooligans. Most of the fans there were members of the official England Travel Club and a large proportion of them there for this game were women and children. They started picking on people for no reason and even attacked a woman with their batons. Flags were torn from the fences and thrown on the floor. I was outraged and thought "I'm not having this", so I dug deep into the pocket of my jeans, pulled out a peseta coin and threw it at a copper's head, but they'd been watching me and spotted straight away, who threw it. They came storming across the rows of empty plastic seats at me and whacked me all over with their truncheons. They dragged me across the seats hitting me on the legs, but they couldn't get me down. I thought to myself "I've had it here, I'm well nicked", but they just beat me black and blue and threw me out of the ground.

The next morning you could see the baton marks on my back. Fucking hell did I ache all over the next day, we had a weekend on the booze in Bilbao and then flew home.

The 94- 95 season, Forest was away at Wimbledon for our last game of the season and it was between our old rivals, Liverpool and us who came third in the newly formed, Premiership. In the end, Blackburn Rovers won it one point ahead of Man United. Me mum, and dad, gave me a lift down in the car and I met up with the rest of our lads down in London. There was no trouble at the game, which we drew 2-2, and it gave us a valuable point to finish three points ahead of the Scousers.

After the game a mob of us headed back into central London and after going in a few pubs and bars we headed back over to Kings Cross. We were well pissed as we'd been on it all day. One of our lads went off for a walk and came rushing back to tell us that a Leeds mob were drinking just around the corner. Four of us left the pub and headed to where they'd been spotted. Almost immediately, we bumped straight into about 15 of them and they came all around us.

"Who the fuck are you?" asked a Leeds midget, straining his neck to look up at me.

"We're Forest so you better do one" I replied. With that short arse shouts across the road.

"Oi Whittaker, get over here," and straight away I recognise this Leeds boy, looking over at us. A few years previously about 30 of us Forest lads had come out of Elland Road after the game and there was a few Leeds lads hanging about giving it the big. We squared up to them and this cunt comes up on my blind side and side-winds me with a punch. Before I can respond the Old Bill are on him and drag him away. A few months later, I'm working on a building site when I get talking to a local lad about the Leeds firm. He then goes on to tell me about one of their main lads named Whittaker, and when he describes him it turns out to be the bloke that clocked me one. It was definitely him to a tee he described as a big lump with a shaved head and a big gob. It turns out that when he was nicked for whacking me he had some kind of drugs on him and ended up getting a bit of bird. Anyway, on this particular night as soon as we see one another we know who each other is, and as soon as he gets near me I try to do him with a head butt, but as he moves backwards to avoid my nut, his legs get tangled up and he falls backwards onto his arse. He'd just lost his balance. I didn't even make contact, but I wish I had. The Old Bill grab me take me to the police station and charge me with threatening behaviour. I'd just got married so that didn't go down too well with the wife. I remember being let out about four hours later and I'd missed the last train home so I had to stay in a grotty little B and B near Kings Cross, which was a right doss hole. When it went to court I was willing to plead guilty to the threatening behaviour charge, but the judge advised me not to. He explained that if I was found guilty of head butting this man then I was looking at a prison sentence, so he advised me to think again about the situation. I looked at my wife who was in court with me, but when I glanced over at her, she burst into tears. "Fucking hell" I thought, "this is all I need". I smiled back as she dabbed at her tears with a tissue. I ended up having to defend myself as I couldn't get legal aid at the time, so I had to cross examine the two coppers who said they saw me head butt a man. One of them was a WPC and I tore her made-up story to shreds. I pointed out to her that if she was stood behind me how could she have possibly seen if I'd pushed him or head butted him or in fact as I'd claimed not even touched him, or whether he had tripped on his own accord. She couldn't answer and even bigger holes began to appear in her very, very, weak, put-together story. The other copper was no better so I was found not guilty and then they read my previous convictions out and I could see by the judge's face that they knew they'd dropped a clanger. I was still put on probation for the threatening behaviour charge after the original hearing was adjourned for social reports. I ended up getting 12 months probation but I accepted that, no problem.

The next time I bumped into Mr. Whittaker was the season after when I took a battle bus full of warriors to Coventry away and if I remember rightly it was the first game of the season, or it was one of the first away games of the season. Anyway, if I'm wrong some sad anorak's sure to take me to task one day over a pint. There was no trouble at Coventry that day and if they have got a mob, I've never seen them, but I have heard from other firms in the Midlands who say that Coventry can pull a good mob on their day. On the same day Leeds were playing at Derby and I just joked with a few of our lads on the bus on the way back home that wouldn't it be funny if Leeds were waiting for us back in Nottingham. "They won't come," "they wouldn't dare come," and "they haven't got the bottle," were just a few of the comments being banded about. We pulled up back in Nottingham and head for The Queens Hotel, which is facing the train station.

"I bet they're in here" I say to Wilmot who's walking just behind me.

"Don't be daft" he laughed, "you're such a wind up".

I walked through the main doors and there they were, about 15 of them sitting around a table. I walked straight over to them.

"All right boys?" I enquired, leaning casually on the back of one of their chairs. Next thing a bottle just misses me head and I back myself out of the doors. A chair then follows just missing my head.

"They're here," I shout at the top of my voice, and our lot still don't believe me. Even Wilmot's trying to work out how I have thrown a chair at myself, then Leeds come out of the pub, see our mob and go back inside and hold the doors. A few of the windows go in and four or five of us try to get in through the back door but my old mate, Whittaker, is doing his best not to let us in. He trades punches with us and does well because if it weren't for him their lot would have got well and truly done. Police sirens fill the air and the blue flashing lights get nearer. It's time to go as we bolt off in all directions.

Eight years on when I was in Wealstun prison I met some Leeds lads in there and we exchanged stories about Mr. Whittaker and they confirmed that he was most definitely one of the main faces at Leeds United and that he was still very active. Before we spoke about my meetings with Mr. Whittaker, they were always inviting me out for drinks, on our release in their home town. After they heard my side of things, they agreed it wouldn't be a good idea to go out on a pub-crawl around Leeds city centre.

Also, in '96 me old mate, Paul Scarrett, sadly died. He'd been living out in Spain on the run from the Old Bill. He was a legend in Nottingham who lived life to the full, and there was a big funeral for him in Arnold. The man was crackers, but he came from a good family and his mum was a magistrate. One of our lads always tells the tale of when Scarrett was a teenager and he dived head first into visiting supporters, from the seats in the old East stand, as they were standing on the terraces, below. About 100 of us turned out to bury him and gave him a good send off. His stepsister was there and I think she was pleased at the send off we gave him. Scarrett became a legend at Forest and on the England scene, and if he were still with us then he could have written a best selling book. Just his exploits with the women alone would have been worth reading about. He loved a bird did Scarrett.

For the Euro '96 game against the Jocks I ran a double decker executive battle bus down to London, and it was full of our lads. The Mansfield lads also ran a bus and we met up at Swiss Cottage. We picked up a Boro lad who was inside with one of our lads. He was hitch hiking down to the game and he told us that Boro were turning out in force. None of us had tickets for the game so we watched it in a pub in Kilburn High Street. There was a good 150 of us there. After the game we ended up in central London at The Globe pub. That fucking Carlisle idiot, Doddy, said in his book that him

NOTTS MAN WITH 40 VIOLENCE CONVICTIONS DIES IN SPAIN

The death of a hooligan fan

By KATE DELAMERE

SOCCER thug Paul Scarrott — jailed 13 times for football hooliganism and with 40 convictions for football violence — has died in Barcelona.

A Foreign Office spokesman today confirmed that the 40-year-old died in hospital on April 30.

A post-mortem examination to establish the cause of death has yet to be performed.

Scarrott — who had the word Forest tattooed on his inner lip — hit national headlines after being booted out of Italy at the start of the World Cup in 1990.

That year he was banned from Nottinghamshire's three professional soccer grounds — Field Mill in Mansfield, Forest's City Ground and Notts County ground Meadow Lane.

Scarrott, who also went under the surname Cooper, last appeared in court last August, after being arrested on the opening day of the new football season, following a clash in a Southampton pub after the Reds' 4-3 victory.

He was the son of a taxi driver and used to work at Calverton Colliery. In 1988, he gave up the job and became a £300-a-week cable layer and part-time bouncer in a Nottingham pub, from which he parted company after disagreements about damage to a gambling machine.

In the summer of 1987, he was convicted at Glasgow of inciting a group of 50 supporters to attack people, including the police.

He was also found guilty of committing a breach of the peace and carrying an offensive weapon.

That summer he was jailed for six months for throwing a beer bottle onto the pitch at the Uefa Cup match between Nottingham Forest and Anderlecht in Brussels.

By 1988, he was reported as having had 19 convictions and been jailed 13 times.

A Foreign Office spokesman said Scarrott's sister, still living in Nottingham, is bringing his body home for a private burial.

She was told of his death by a local police officer. Unconfirmed reports suggest he died after taking a steroid overdose.

TERROR OF THE TERRACES: Paul Scarrott

Sad loss of Paul

MAY 10 proved to be a sad day for me. That's when I learned of the death of Paul Scarrott.

I read the reports in newspapers with dismay. Yes, Paul had been a football hooligan, but he also had a wonderful side, which I had the pleasure of knowing.

Paul, without drugs or drink, was a kind, caring, hardworking human being, with lots of love to give.

He faced up to his addiction problem last year, but unfortunately returned to drinking some months later. Paul wasn't a bad man, just an ill one.

SADIE CROMPTON
Craven Road
Hyson Green

and his cronies had it with 150 Forest and it went toe-to-toe. Total bollocks! Your fucking cheap perm must have fallen in your eyes and obscured your view. What really happened was, we walked around outside the pub looking for Jocks. A few lads came out the pub and words were exchanged. It would have been no contest and we are not bullies like some teams so we left it and jumped back on the tube, but old dickhead, Doddy boy, saw it different. England's No 1? My arse! It's pure fiction. The coppers were there, watching, so we, as I say, left it. We tried to get into Trafalgar Square but the Old Bill sussed us and fucked us off out of it. Ten of us went back and somehow we got through onto the square. Some Jock casuals were leaning up against the railing and I went over to them and asked who they were.

"Who are you?" came back the reply in a thick Scottish accent.

"We're Forest".

"We're Dundee," and with that one of them launches a full beer can that hits me straight in the face. I pull my belt off and crack one of them in the face with the buckle. The coppers split it up and herd us up the road. The Jocks knew that if they came out of that square then they were going to get well done. Within minutes, my eye's swelled up until it was nearly closed and I knew I'd have a shiner the next day. That's the Jocks party trick, throwing full cans in your face. We got in a pub out of the way and everyone had their mobile phones to their ears but there was no real trouble the rest of the night. I heard that Chelsea had a few boys out that night but the Old Bill prevented it from going off.

Scarrott on the far right and my mate gez Mullen left at back (both sadly gone).

Part 5

ASTON VILLA'S firm hasn't often come to Forest but the time they came about 50 handed they got slaughtered, big time on the bridge. I didn't go to the game but the lads that went said that if it weren't for the coppers they would have been thrown into the Trent, something that over the years 'as happened to a good many visiting supporters.

The second time they came, I'd been out collecting deposits from the lads for a forthcoming bus trip down to Tottenham. About 30 of us were drinking in a pub near Notts County's ground when the riot Old Bill pulled up and came in and nick the lot of us, took us away and lock us up. We'd not seen a Villa fan all day and don't even know if they had a firm out, or if they were in town. We were arrested on a Prevention Order and let out that night about 9 o'clock.

I hadn't been having a good time lately. My wife of two years upped and left me. She came home one day and said she was going home to her mum's and that she needed a break from me. I fucked off to America to see my sister who, at the time, was still living out there. I went out to spend New Years Eve with her so I flew out on Christmas day. When I got there, I had a problem with my passport and with a visa from a previous trip. The last time I'd been out there their Immigration had forgotten to take out a green slip stapled into my passport, which in effect meant that I was still in the country and had not left on my last visit. I'd booked a hotel in Las Vegas for me and me sister because I'd just split up with my wife and she was separated from her American husband. I had all the Christmas presents for her from mum and dad and the rest of the family but here I was but unable to get into the country. After taking my passport away and then leading me off into a side room, I was informed by an official that I was an illegal alien. They did eventually believe that it was just a simple mistake on their behalf but this one Hispanic woman official amongst them just went off on one, and was like a pit bull terrier and wouldn't let it drop. She stared straight into my eyes and snarled, showing her manky teeth, and with dried up spit resting in each corner of her bee-stung lips, spat "you're going nowhere until we've checked you out".

I could hear her on the phone talking to someone and the word "hooligan" seemed to be coming up in the conversation quite a bit. A man came out, spoke to me, and informed me that Immigration had spoken to the F.B.I. and that they had a file on me, which included my plans to cause riots at the forthcoming Olympic games.

"Don't you mean the World Cup?" I asked.

"No, the Olympic Games", he replied.

They were a bit late. The football World Cup had been held in the States in '94 and I knew if England had of qualified there was no way I'd have been let into the country. But the Olympics? What the fuck was that all about? Anyway, they told me I was to be deported and put on the first available flight back to England. I was also told that if I wanted to get back into the U.S.A. at a later date then I must go to the American Embassy in London and have an interview which would decide whether I would be allowed back in. I was photographed, and finger printed and taken to the departure gate for my flight back to Heathrow. I then had my passport handed over to a stewardess and was told to wait, until they were ready for me to board the aircraft, I was called over the public address system by a woman's voice, which said, "we are waiting for a deportee to board this flight". Everyone sitting in the departure lounge looked at me as I stood up and walked towards the boarding gate. I think after that announcement everyone there knew who the deportee was. I was escorted onto the plane and made to sit with two empty seats either side of me. This was the days before blind- folds and orange jump suits but this was still punishment U.S.A. style, even though I'd done absolutely nothing wrong. The plane I was going home on was the one I'd landed on a few hours before, but on the way over, I wasn't being treated like a criminal. Once we were up in the air all the other people around me were drinking and eating, and were being asked by the flight crew if they were all right and were they comfortable. No one said a word to me or offered me a meal or a drink so I opened the pack of beers I'd taken out for my sister and cracked a can open. A stewardess came rushing over.

"No No" she shouted, "You can't drink that if it hasn't been purchased from the cabin crew". Anyway to cut a long story short she gave me a couple of beers and as I queued to use the toilet a bloke came over to me.

"Are you a Nottingham Forest fan?" he asked. I nodded a yes.

"I thought I recognised ya, and when I noticed the Timberland boots and the Armani jeans I just knew you were a football fan and I knew I knew your face from somewhere". He went on to tell me that he was a big Forest fan and that he knew people that I knew. He was originally from Tamworth in the Midlands and used to sit in the "A" block at the City ground. He was now living in Kansas and was on his way back to England to visit relatives. I couldn't believe it. A Forest fan had fucking recognised me. We sat together for a couple of hours and had a right old chat about our Club. When we landed, I got my passport back at Customs, and was free to go. My sister when she found out what had happened went mad and told me I should complain about it. The thing was they had me down as an undesirable person so what could I really do about it?

Back at home I ran a battle bus to an away game up at Sunderland. We'd had a bit of grief a few seasons earlier so this was a bit of revenge mission, plus I don't like Sunderland anyway. I filled the bus no problem but to be honest there was only about 15 good lads I could rely on it if it kicked off. The rest were just bodies to fill the bus up with, sort of wannabees. It was basically, a money making scheme and a chance to blood a few young Herberts in battle. We left Nottingham early for the three-hour drive North. When we arrived in Sunderland at midday we parked just around the corner from The Wheatsheaf pub, which is one of Sunderland's main boozers. Me and Palmer and a few of the Mansfield lads who'd travelled up with us, headed towards The Wheatsheaf half expecting to find none of Sunderland's mob out this early. It was a nice, sunny day and to our amazement sitting outside, enjoying the sun and sitting having a few beers were a lot of their lads. We stopped, looked at one another, and with no Old Bill around, went straight into them. They threw a few glasses and bottles at us, and we picked up some pint glasses and threw them at them and they then backed off into the doorway of the pub and it went toe-to-toe as they tried to hold us off. The rest of our lot were still getting off the coach totally unaware that we were having a right old battle with the Mackems. We had them backing off and shitting themselves, and it was their entire Seaburn Casual mob. What we didn't realise was the pub had quite a few entrances and exits so in no time at all the ones inside were coming from behind us with pool cues, bottles, and bar stools. You name it; they were holding it as a weapon. We weren't that bothered because we knew that the other 50 lads were sure to be here soon to back us up. Next thing is me mate, Alex, who's fighting alongside me, gets a glass straight in his boat race and there's blood pissing out everywhere. We had to now retreat a bit. We didn't leg it, we just backed off a little bit as pool balls and bottles came our way. We just needed that little bit of space between them and us so we could get a second breath and go again. Anyway, the rest of the lads would arrive soon surely? What the fuck had happened to them?" I'm thinking. The Mackems fancied it now, and came at us in one big wave and ran what was left of us everywhere. I ended up behind enemy lines watching Sunderland chasing our lads up the road. I had to jump some railings to get away after I was spotted mingling in with them but it turned out we would have been waiting forever for our back up to get to us because as soon as we had kicked it off with the Sunderland lads and they started to get the upper hand then the idiots I'd filled the bus up with decided to fuck off a bit sharpish. They did one with the driver of the bus, who put his foot down and fucked off out of it. I've never been so embarrassed in all my life as we were backed off all the way to the Weir Bridge. We made a bit of a stand and a couple of their front runners were decked and took a bit of a kicking on the floor but we were off again as the rest of their lads caught us up and run us again. Fuck me, it was so embarrassing. The police turned up and got it together but it was too late for us, we must have been run a good mile and a half; it's a pity we weren't doing the run for a charity because we would have raised a nice few quid, the distance we ran. It was shameful to see. The Old Bill found us a pub in the town centre and in there already unscathed was the rest of the coach. I was fucking fuming. I was going fucking mad. A few of our coppers came in the pub and they'd already heard we'd been humiliated and by the looks on their faces you could just tell that they wanted to say something. Just before kick-off, we were escorted out of the pub and off towards the ground but we had to walk back past the pub where we'd come unstuck. As we passed, they were all still outside drinking and we had to walk straight through the middle of them as they sang, "Run, Run, Run Away". They were on both sides of us with the Old Bill holding them back.

"Piss off" I shouted back as I held my head high. They laughed and gave us the wankers sign.

After the game, I was still fuming but now we had a few more top faces with us, I knew now that things would be different. I still had the hump and as soon, as one of them Mackem cunts started gobbing off in me face, outside, I just punched him and decked him. The Old Bill jumped on me and took me off to the police station down in the town centre. Me and another Forest kid, who'd also been nicked, were let out about 8.30 at night. We'd missed the bus back to Nottingham, and there were no trains back home and to tell you the truth it was a bit dodgy hanging around in Sunderland, so we jumped in a cab back to Newcastle, which cost us £12. I ended up pulling a bird in Julies Nightclub and booked a room for £70 in The Royal Station Hotel. I spent the night shagging her and she told me she was a student studying at the university and that she was on a bit of a break.

"Why don't you come back to Nottingham?" I asked. She thought about it for what must have been all of two seconds, smiled and said "Alright", and that was it. We went back to her house in Chester-le-Street to pick up some belongings. She lived with her mum and dad who I think wasn't that put out that their little baby doll was off travelling. They didn't even come out the house to wave her off, nice family? Nice girl? We'd agreed a £130 fare with a local cab driver to take us back to Nottingham, which worked out cheaper and quicker than the train. As soon as we get back to Nottingham, we dropped our gear off at my house and go straight down to The Greyhound, which is my local pub. Our Main Man comes in the pub and spots me in the pub with her.

"I don't believe it" he says to a mate of mine, "That Clarke goes up there, gets arrested and brings one back with him". He has a dry sense of humour 'as our Main Man. She stayed with me for a week before I put her on a National Express coach back home. While she was stopping with me my ex-wife phoned up to speak to me about something and when this girl answered the phone, my ex went fucking ballistic. Well, she was still the wife at the time because technically we weren't yet divorced.

"What's she doing in my house?" she ranted to me down the phone, I think that was the final straw, I think after that, there was no chance of a reconciliation. To tell the truth I was getting a bit sick of the student after a few days but when I came home from work she'd have a dinner ready for me so she wasn't such a bad girl and in the looks stakes I'd give her 6 out of 10. I took her out on the piss every night but I think I was getting a bit bored, so she had to go. She came down to see me again one other time but it just fizzled out. When I had to go back to court, for whacking the geezer outside the ground. I picked the Forest youth up, who was in the nick with me, and we travelled up there in my van, and before I left I checked the engine oil and water but like a fucking idiot I must have put too much oil in the engine and overfilled it. I was doing 70-80 m.p.h. and as I came off at the services near Durham I braked a bit sharp and the oil must have come up from the engine and caused a fire under the bonnet. As I pulled over the van was on fire, luckily enough some coppers were parked nearby and came to my rescue, and used a fire extinguisher to put the flames out. This was about 9.30 a.m. and I told the coppers that I was on my way to court in Sunderland, so they phoned up for me and told the magistrate's court that I was going to be late and explained the situation to them. The A.A. came out and somehow managed to replace a few wires that had melted and burned out. Surprisingly the fire hadn't caused too much damage. I got to the court at midday and went straight in. I pleaded guilty to threatening behaviour and to my surprise they never read out any of my previous convictions. The judge looked at me and gave me a £150 fine. I had to stop myself from smiling as he peered over his glasses at me. I couldn't believe it. That was a result. That'll do me. I could live with that. I thought I was going to get banned, again. The judge had said, prior to sentencing me that I'd incurred a great deal of cost already, what with having to take a day off work, and my van breaking down. So he turned out to be a decent fella in my eyes and had done the decent thing by only giving me a fine which, as I say, I was more than happy with.

The Dam.

Lille B4 Colombia, France 1998.

Daft England band, France 1998, with Gary Newbon.

Tunisia game, France 1998,
Marsielles.

Marsielle 1998, B4 game.
A few of the Mansfield lads.

Toulouse Square B4
Romania game 1998.

Malmo, away with Forest back in Europe, hooligans dream.

Malmo A, back in Europe.

Our mob, Finland away with England.

Part 6

WE HAD Birmingham City away in a League game in the 97/98 season and the lads had got a pub sorted right in the heart of Zulu land. I had to miss the game. as my estranged wife had been knocked down by a car, after leaving a nightclub in the early hours of the morning she was on a life support machine for a week and was in a pretty bad way, I was worried sick and it was touch and go if she would survive, so I didn't want to go too far from her.

The boys had only been in the pub five minutes when a group of black lads came in and it kicked off in the doorway of the pub. Our lot have backed them up and then run them up the road. Minutes later they were back again but this time they were tooled up to the eyeballs. A lot of our lads got hurt that day and I mean hurt badly. We weren't just fighting Birmingham City's Zulus but the scumbags and Herberts off the run down council estate the pub was situated on, a couple of the lads were cut badly and one was knocked unconscious after he had a paving slab dropped on his head. To me doing something like that is not in the rules of combat. A few of the lads started arriving back at The Greyhound pub in Arnold around about 8.30 that evening and they looked like the walking wounded from Rourkes Drift. Well, they had been fighting the Zulus all day.

Not the following season but the one after that, we played them again and I made sure I was there this time. About 80 of us caught the service train and we got there about 2 o'clock. One or two of our main faces didn't come with us for reasons best known to them. We came out of New Street Station and their mob was standing outside a pub, just up the hill. We ran towards them but before a punch was thrown the Old Bill arrived and got in between the two mobs then turned us around and escorted us to the ground. After the game, there was no real bother as we were herded back to the station, under a heavy police escort.

At the home game against them, they didn't show up but we turned out big for them. I rate Birmingham and they're no mugs but I think they have to look how a few of their lads behave.

France '98 in the World Cup finals saw England in Group G with Romania, Tunisia and Colombia. I went out to France for the two weeks of the finals and me, me sister, Sean and his misses, and a few others rented a villa just outside Avignon. It cost near on £3,000 and was surrounded by vineyards and rolling hills. It was the bollocks, pure luxury.

On the day of the first game, we left the girls at the villa and headed into Marseille for the Tunisia game. It was a boiling hot June day with clear blue skies. We met up with a few lads and learnt there'd been trouble between England fans and the locals, who were mostly Arab or black, the night before. We headed off towards the stadium after a few beers and saw the odd scuffle here and there but nothing to write home about. We got tickets for the game, which England won 2-0. Afterwards about 15 of us had a few beers near the stadium and then caught the Metro down to the old port. When we came out onto the street there was Arabs both sides of us spitting and shouting and throwing things at us.

"Come on you Arab bastards", I shouted, walking towards them, fists clenched, but the cowardly cunts backed off knowing that if I'd have thrown a punch then the French Old Bill, who were standing there watching, would have nicked me and not them. The Old Bill cleared them off and we found a little back street bar out of the way.

After a while, the Mansfield lads who were with us wanted to turn it in for the night and head off back to their hotel. Me and me mate said it was about time we headed back to the villa so we set off with the others to look for a cab to take us the hour's drive home. As we walked up the road, some nutty Arab cunt came out of the shadows and tries to crack me across the nut with a bottle. He misses me and he backs off. I whip my leather belt off, wrap it around my knuckles and smashed him in the face with the big, heavy buckle. It does the trick as he staggers off into the night having had a taste of the Gary Clarke party trick which, over the years I've perfected down to a fine art. I just know though that one day, as I whip my belt off, my trousers are going to end up around my ankles! Anyway, in the end it was fucking well dodgy in Marseille but just to prove a point I took my shirt off and stuck it in the rucksack I had on my back, and walked around the streets bare-chested, proud to be English as I showed off the three lions

I have tattooed on my chest. We got some right looks but I didn't give a fuck.

Back at the villa we'd wander in the local bar, which was a mile from us. The locals were sound but looked at us at times like we were from another planet. We went in there one night after a day of swimming and diving in and out of the villa's pool and France were playing. As we walked in you could have heard a pin drop as a deafening silence fell over the place.

The next England game was against Romania in Toulouse, which was a three-hour drive away. I'd got pissed the day before and had an argument and a bit of a fall-out with Sean so the drive there was a bit frosty. We met Dale and about 30 of the Forest lads who'd been staying down in Lorrett in Spain and had come up to France for the game. In the main square, we had a good laugh, as most of the England fans were just there to enjoy themselves. The touts were having a field day and were selling tickets for this game for £300 and you couldn't get them for love or money. I said "fuck that, I aint paying that sort of money for a ticket," so we watched it in a bar near the ground with some of the Mansfield lads. I got absolutely steaming drunk and started arguing with Sean again. England had lost the game and I had the right fucking hump. I'd also been on the wacky baccy so I was itching for a row with someone so Sean fucked off and left me. It was my own fault because I was being a right daft cunt. He ended up driving back to the villa on his own while I found a nice uncomfy park bench to sleep off my hangover.

The next morning I bumped the train to Avignon and caught a taxi from there back to the villa. I'd been to Avignon before as I'd stopped off there on my way back from Italia '90. I had been to visit a mate of mine who was in the Foreign Legion and they have a base there. It's a beautiful place and is well worth a visit. When I got back I apologised to Sean for being an idiot and we made it up. I'd made a right cunt of myself and the whole situation was my fault.

The last game in Group G was against Colombia in Lens. There'd been more rows at the villa, mostly with my sister, and for me it was time to go so me and one of me mates decided to clear off to Paris and have a night out. From there, we went on to Lille and met me old mate, Ashley White, who was doing an interview for Sky television. He'd come over from Prague where he now lives and works. Tickets for the game were going for £300 and I wouldn't pay that so I watched it in a bar with Palmer and a few of the Mansfield lads. We beat the Colombians 2-0 and four days later, we played Argentina in St. Etienne but by this time, I'd had enough and watched the game on T.V. back home in The Greyhound Pub. In the end we lost to the Argies on penalties but if we had have won and gone through to the next stage we would have played Holland and I definitely would have gone back out there for that one. Dale, one of our main boys at Forest, got stopped at East Midlands airport and was turned back trying to travel out for the Argentina game. That was my story of the World Cup. I think we had more trouble amongst ourselves at the villa than there was at any of the England games.

My next England game was in Hungary. I flew out to see my mate, Ashley, in Prague for a couple of days. He is a major England fan, he likes to get dressed up for the games in an England robe, and he carries a big, plastic gold coloured World Cup. He's not a thug or one of the chaps but cross him at your peril. He's no mug, that's for sure. He's a handy lad but just a pure football fan. There was about 500 England fans that made the trip out there for this meaningless, friendly that finished in a 1-1 draw. Even the Hungarians didn't seem that keen as the crowd was only twenty thousand. There was a bit of trouble on the Underground before and after the game but I didn't see any of it. I didn't get into any bother, a bit different from when we played France in Paris at their new national stadium, 15 of us went out there on the Euro star, including Scouse Dave and a couple of the Darlo lads. We met up with a few more Forest lads and had a few pints in 'The Roast Beef' pub. The place was packed and after a while the 200 England shirts that were in there and standing outside on the pavement, started getting a bit boisterous. All the usual songs started stuff like Rule Britannia and anti I.R.A. songs. The next thing they're throwing bottles at the local Africans walking past. We could see where this is heading as the locals start to mob up at the end of the road, closely watched by the French riot police. We don't want to get caught up in this so we decided to go off in search of quieter surroundings. We turned off into a side street and bump straight into 50 locals. We couldn't avoid one another. We just fell into each other and it was game on. We backed them off with a flurry of punches and one of them came at me swinging a plank of wood, but he missed me by a mile. A mate of mine was badly cut on the hand by one of them with a knife. The row went on for about 15 minutes with them coming at us and us standing our ground and not budging, and them backing off. They'd wave their knives about and try to slash and cut you and they'd throw things at you, but they wasn't willing to trade punches with you and have a proper tear-up toe-to-toe. The police arrived and we casually walked away, like nothing had happened, but as we looked back the street was strewn with debris, broken glass, bricks and timber. You name it, it covered the road. We were lucky, or unlucky to have actually had this row depending on how you look at it because when we came out of the Paris railway station earlier on that day, a policeman from Nottingham, who was on England duty as a spotter, clocked us as we walked past him, he done no more than gave us a wink and a knowing nod of his head and let us go on our way. In March 2000 my dear old Nan died she'd been ill with cancer of the bowel and she'd hid it from everyone. She was in hospital and having a high dose of morphine to ease the pain, she was in. On the Saturday night she was up, and dancing and singing old war songs and was back to looking and sounding her old self, but next day she had a relapse and suffered a heart attack and over the next 24 hours she slipped away. I was at her bedside when she went and held her hand as I said my last goodbyes to her. That lady was so special to me and was a real diamond. I could do no wrong in her eyes and I've lost count of the times she had bailed me out of trouble. All the boys at Forest knew her well and I even took her into the pub with all the lads on more than one occasion, she was a real larger than life character who I miss so much, and she's still talked about to this day. Grandma I love you so much and things aint been the same since you left. God bless you, your forever in our hearts. xxx

Ouside Celic,up the Rangers.

Athens, Greece away with England.

Me and Sheffield John outside Ibrox

Our firm in Athens.

In London on tour.

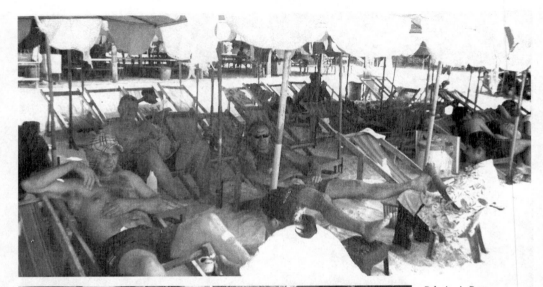

Relaxing in Pattaya.

In the Dogs, Pattaya with my mate from Cardiff H.

Forest's youth firm F.N.S.

After our release from the cells, Derby away.
Left to right: Mick (Plymouth), Dale C., Nickys (now in Torquay), Parma and me.

My mate Jonny S. from Newcastle in Thailand – Top man.

Finland away, bit cold.

CHAPTER 9

The Mackems Don't Mackem Like Me

MY MATE JOHN from Sheffield had been going out with a lovely Geordie girl and then he split up with her and had to find somewhere to live, so he moved in with a lad who was one of the boys in the Newcastle firm. Through John, I became friends with some of their boys and I started going up there quite a bit.

One weekend I went up there and they were playing Sunderland away and anybody who knows anything about football rivalries will tell ya that these two teams hate one another with a passion. For this particular game the Newcastle, lads had hired a bus to come down from Scotland on the pretence that they were going for a day out at the races. They had it all worked out so that they took all the back roads so that their route wouldn't draw the attention of the Old Bill. The first pub we came to in Sunderland we were straight off the bus and was in there drinking. A lot of the Geordies older lot went in by train. The police soon learned that there was 80 of us drinking in the pub and swooped on us. Words were exchanged and bottles were thrown, so they decided on the spot to arrest the whole pub, which they did, and they held us until 11 o'clock that night. The lads that went by train had it right off as they had running battles with the Mackems all the way to the ground. I could hear what was going on from the police radios as I sat handcuffed in the back of the police van. We were all released without charge but the Old Bill weren't best pleased when they knew I was from Nottingham. They saw me as a troublemaker and someone that had gone up there purely for the bother. I just told them I was a Newcastle United fan from Nottingham but I don't think they believed me. I was gutted as I missed out on a good night out in Newcastle, but I had a rather pleasant night in the cells so I can't complain.

England out in Helsinki was my next adventure, 25 Forest lads went out there to watch a boring 0-0 draw in a World Cup qualifier and at £4 a pint it aint the cheapest place to go out on the piss, a bit different from Estonia, which is cheap at 50p a pint.

On the fashion front it seems that anyone that wants to be or thinks that they've one of the chaps at football dress's in an item of Stone Island clothing, be it a jumper, jacket, coat, sweatshirt, or jeans. That little badge on the arm means so much to some people and some people have just discovered it. I can remember in Nottingham the so called fashionable, "in" people wearing Stone Island T shirts in the late 80s and then it seemed to fade out a bit, and then the football people picked up on it and it came back even stronger. Now you can find it in almost every High Street men's shop and even some mail order catalogues are selling it. You wait until the Derby mob discovers it in a few years' time. It'll be the smartest they've been for years. They can throw away their Donkey jackets then!

One of our lads works at East Midlands airport so he got a few of us cheap flights out to Poland for a European Championship qualifier. He also sorted us out the same hotel in Warsaw as the flight crew stayed in. When we got there it turned out that the England team were also staying at the same hotel. We had a couple of drinks and got chatting to some high-up people at Ipswich Town, and a big-time, high-ranking official from Aston Villa came over.

"Ah, the gentlemen of the press, how nice to see you!"

Dale, one of our main lads, cut him short.

"No, we're Cloughie's boys".

That didn't put him off as he handed us all a metal F.A. pin badge. One of the lads who'd been boozing a bit too much on the flight over was starting to get a bit wobbly on his legs, and his speech was slurred and was half way to getting pissed and then he started knocking the champagne down his neck straight from the bottle, so that sort of behaviour didn't go down too well with the hotel management, and we ended up being told that we'd have to find somewhere else to stay, though we did stay in the bar for the rest of the evening but kept our heads down and had a quiet trouble free drink.

The next morning the word on the street was that a mob of Poles had attacked the English fans drinking in 'Champions Bar' the previous night. Everyone arranged to meet back in there that afternoon so we went off to have some breakfast. We noticed in a few shops and bars just how much prices had gone up since the last time we were out there and the price of beer and food had almost doubled. It had become more Westernised and caught up with the rest of Europe. As we walked down to a little café, a bottle sailed through the air and landed, smashing at our feet. Across the other side of the road was 15 or so Poles dressed in leather jackets and they were all big lumps that looked like they could handle themselves. The traffic was that busy they couldn't find a gap in the cars to come across at us. We exchanged words and hurled abuse and hand gestures and we carried on up the road, but after that incident, I just knew it was going to be one of those days.

Back in 'Champions Bar' there was about 100 strong English mob with lads from Huddersfield and Sheffield, all talking about the row with the Poles the night before. A German lad came in who I later learned was named Ronald, and he apparently goes around Europe following and organising rows between clubs. He's poked his nose into so many fights between clubs, Arsenal, P.S.G., Ajax, Feynoord, Valencia, and Barcelona. He's been everywhere, even Millwall v West Ham. At one time, he hung around with Chelsea's firm and was good mates with Fat Pat. He's a walking A-Z of European football hooliganism but some people say he's a shit-stirring cunt. He tells everyone in the pub that the Poles are up the road waiting for us in a park and that there's no Old Bill, with them. The pub empties and the English set off to find them.

"Let's just finish our drinks first" said Dale, looking at his glass because someone had just got another round in. One of the Mansfield lads, Blowey, went off with them. It was only 3 o'clock and to be honest us Forest lot thought that as usual rumour control had gone into overdrive and some people had, had too much Marching Powder up their noses and were getting a bit paranoid. We half expected them to all walk back into the pub in a couple of minutes having found no Poles. We drank up and was probably only five minutes behind the main lot. Blowey called us up on his mobile and told us the park was just near the Fugi building. We could see that so we headed in that direction. As we came to the park the English mob were running towards us. We thought the Polish police were chasing them.

"What's happening?" I asked a couple of lads sprinting past us.

No one stopped to answer as we pushed our way through a tide of rushing bodies. A herd of gazelles being chased by a hungry lion sprang to mind. When we got to the park gates we could see a mob of Poles and they came towards us as soon as they came within striking distance we stood and traded blows with them and with the help of a couple of Wigan lads we held our own. Dustbins and bricks came at us and one big Pole was flashing a huge blade around. I copped a bin on my nut, which opened my head wide open. There was claret everywhere. Now the tide was turning as we backed the Poles off, and soon they were on their toes as we ran them back into the park. The rest of the England lads came back and we completely turned the whole situation around. The Old Bill arrived and I had to get out of the way as I was coverered in blood. A few lads had been badly injured before we got there. Blowey was beaten black and blue and had two black eyes. One lad was stabbed in the leg, and Dodger from Sheffield United got an axe in his head. The England boys had gone for a straight row but we were well set up as lots of the Poles had weapons. Apparently there was pictures of the fight on the net within an hour. We all went our separate ways, as there was Old Bill everywhere.

The next time I saw everybody was outside the ground before the kick-off. I had a ticket for the match and inside the ground we were right next to a fenced off piece of "no-man's land," which was all that was between us, and the Poles. A few lads shook the fence and leaned on it until it collapsed, and we then went across the no mans land bit of terracing and into the Poles. It was toe-to-toe as we lent across the fence whacking them. One of them was waving a long blade about as he tried to slash and cut me. That was it, time for my party trick as off came my leather belt, I quickly wrapped it around my clenched fist before I let him have it straight in the face and around the side of his head, the Old Bill moved in and lashed out with their batons. The Poles had no class they were dressed like extras from the 70s T.V. programmes the Sweeney or Minder. If they didn't have the shaved head, they had the Dennis Waterman hairdo.

At the next Forest home game our copper who been out in Poland as a spotter, came up to me and asked if I was an idiot.

"I can't believe you" he said, "You're lucky to not be on the front page of every newspaper".

My mate from Liverpool had C.S. gassed all the press and the cameraman down at the front so they couldn't take any pictures of the fighting so how lucky was I? After the final whistle in Poland, which finished in a 0-0 draw, it was a bit dodgy out on the streets so we had a few beers in the bar at the Marriot Hotel. There was bouncers on the door so that none of the locals could get in. The Poles were running around the streets mob-handed looking for the English. In the bar we got chatting to the journalist, Rob Sheppard, and we drank with him until the early hours. He was quite interested in what had gone on with the Poles and asked me if I'd be interested in doing a T.V. interview. I wasn't interested as I had caked blood on the back of my head from me heading metal dustbins in the park. Radio Five Live also wanted me to do a live broadcast but I turned down their offer of stardom. In the basement of the hotel was a disco and down there, we got chatting with football commentators John Motson and Ray Stubbs and two nice fellas they are to. We had a good chat about football with both of them.

For the World Cup qualifier against Germany in Munich, Forest had about 70 lads out there and I was arsehole lucky to get out there. The Notts police kept coming around my house a couple of weeks before the game to serve a civil banning order on me. The Old Bill had been ringing me up and leaving messages but I was either out or at work or just not opening the door to them. In the end, I rang our football copper and he explained that it wasn't Nottingham police bringing the banning order on me, but Derbyshire police because of the trouble I'd been involved in out in Greece. I trusted our copper who was a half decent geezer, and over the years, he'd turned a blind eye, to certain things and had let some things go. This whole, civil banning order had all come about because of a spot of bother I'd had with an England spotter from the Derbyshire Constabulary. I'd gone for a week's holiday on the Greek Island of Agenia with my sister, and a mate. The bulk of the Forest lads were staying on another island in the resort of Falaraki. I went for the quieter option. I knew I wouldn't last the pace with the other lot.

On the day of the game I got the boat to the mainland and met up with the rest of the lads in one of the squares, which was packed with bars. About 30 of us caught the metro and for some reason we got off two stops before the stadium and went for a few more beers. The place was swarming with Greek fans and we tried to get on the tube but we couldn't get on, it was that busy. Words were exchanged with some Greeks and the next thing punches were thrown. We eventually got on the train and as we pulled in at the stop for the Olympic stadium the platform was full of Greeks waiting for us. As we went down the stairs they were all around us and above us, spitting at us. I lobbed a bottle into them and the whole lot went up as it went fucking mental on the stairs. They were as game as fuck and kept on coming at us. The Old Bill intervened and escorted us out of the station. It was pitch black by now and you couldn't see a thing, but you could hear things hitting the ground as the Greeks hurled missiles at us in the darkness. We were walking a gauntlet as the Greek Old Bill led us through them. One or two of our lot, got hit with things but you just had to keep going. The Greek Old Bill didn't seem that bothered about nicking any locals but that's the price, you pay for being an Englishman abroad watching football. They wouldn't come into us and have a fistfight. They weren't that brave. They were cocky little shits who knew we'd fucking muller them, if they did. As we got near the ground one of our lot pointed out the Derby copper that had sent me a letter 6 months before, telling me not to come to Derby County's ground for an England v Mexico International. A few lads gave him a bit of abuse and we walked towards him. He was with a group of English spotters and some Greek coppers who were filming us with a video camera. Someone threw a punch at one of the English coppers as his camcorder ended up on the floor as the punch missed, luckily or unluckily. Anyway, these spotters were then legged across the car park. The Greek police came over and calmed it down and even they were finding it hard to keep a straight face as our plain-clothes police spotters disappeared into the distance. So, basically someone somewhere had it in for me with this banning order and as our copper at Forest had said, it wasn't them who wanted to serve it on me.

The night before we were due to fly out to Germany from Stanstead for the England game in Munich, the Old Bill managed to serve this civil banning order on me. My mate from Newcastle was staying the night with me. I was upstairs getting ready to go out and he was downstairs watching telly while waiting for me. Then there was a knock on the front door and he opens it, and lets this big lad in, and he thinks this bloke is a mate of mine I put my head over the top of stairs and standing at the bottom is one of our match coppers. He says he knows we are planning on going to Germany but lets me know that whichever way we are thinking of going, they will stop me. I wasn't due in court until the following week but I told him I was going to take my chances on going out to Germany, no matter what he said.

The next day we set off to Stanstead airport for the flight to Germany. Suckkiy, one of our lads, had laid on a bus and the rest of us travelled down by car. When we arrived, there was Old bill everywhere at passport control. I knew I wasn't going to get passed them and through the customs check point. There looked to be no way past them and I knew in my heart that I was going to get stopped and turned back. They was stopping everyone and checking their passports but I stood there and worked out that every few seconds there'd be a lapse in their concentration as they checked their records against the passport they were inspecting and that was my signal to go. "Go," said me mate Eddie, as a gap appeared, and he covered me by blocking their view and to my surprise I was through. I couldn't believe it but the funny thing was, and at the time I felt terrible about it, they stopped me mate Eddie from Newcastle. Later they took him to court in Chelmsford and put a banning order on him.

The flight took off with me on it and later that evening there was about 70 of us that met up in Frankfurt in an Irish bar. We moved off to an area called Saxon Housen where there's, quite a few different bars, but we noticed that the German police were following us around and were basically, checking up on us. We were having a quiet drink in one of the Old Town bars when this German youth came up to me and asked if we would like to fight. "We meet you at 8 o'clock tonight in the Irish bar opposite the main train station," he said.

"Yeah, great mate, we'll be there" I replied, and off he went. It was like I'd just arranged a date with a bird. He was so polite and to the point. Kraut efficiency at its best! We all made our way back to the Irish bar in dribs and drabs, and true to their word 100 of them showed up. It turned out that they were made up of three different German sides, Enintracht Frankfurt, some German third division team and another tin-pot Kraut side, but dead on eight they were outside the bar calling for us to come out. We came steaming out and they went everywhere before a punch was thrown. We chased them all over town and at one point we even went back to the bar to grab a drink. It was thirsty work chasing Germans. As we downed our well-earned pints I notice a few of their lot gathering on a corner just near the pub. A handful of us done a pincer movement and came out the back door of the pub and sneaked up behind them. They were gone in a flash as the chase was back on. We went back into the Irish bar and the Old Bill turned up so we moved off to another bar and the Krauts came back again and tried to attack the pub. It was the same old story, every time we came out they'd leg it. Two of ours, Michael Johnson and Blowy got nicked.

Next day we were off to Munich and on our arrival, we plotted up in a bar near the train station, but I was well paranoid about the Old Bill. I had a ticket for the match but I was that worried about getting nicked I sold my match ticket to a Newcastle lad that I knew for £100 and me and Chelsea Mark sat in the train station and watched it on the big screen. I was a bit worried that if I'd gone to the match then I was sure to get nicked but I was gutted I hadn't kept my ticket when we eventually won 5-1. We didn't get to Munich until about 5 o'clock so we'd missed all the aggro that was shown on T.V. We'd already had our fun in Frankfurt the night before and I was well aware that I was probably a target for the German Old Bill. To tell you the truth I didn't really see any English Old Bill out there but when I got back home, they let it be known that I'd been spotted out there.

On the Wednesday after the Germany game we had Albania in a game up at Newcastle. I was due in court in Nottingham on the Thursday morning for this civil banning order so I got my solicitor to phone up the court and tell them I was on holiday. I went up to Newcastle the night before the game and stayed with mates as I did actually have a week off of work. On the day of the game, I met up with the Forest lads in The Adelphi pub with some the Newcastle lads and we've having a drink when in walks the Forest match copper and a Newcastle copper.

"I thought you were on holiday," they said.

"I am" I replied, "I'm on holiday in Newcastle".

The next day my solicitor went to court, and pleaded not guilty on my behalf, and he got the case adjourned until September. At that time in 2001, if you lost a civil case against a banning order you didn't have to pay the costs, since then, they have changed the law and if you now plead not guilty and are found guilty then you have to pay costs. It finally went to court in the December, and 6 coppers turned up to give evidence against me. There was a Plymouth copper, a Stoke copper, a Birmingham copper, a Liverpool copper, a Notts copper, and the Derby copper who stood up and said that he feared for his safety as a postcard had been sent to his home address with a picture of a face looking over a wall with the words "watching you". I hadn't sent it and that's the honest truth but I still got the blame for it, they showed me on their video out in Greece gobbing off at him and basically I was convicted after every copper that was called to give evidence against me said that they knew me from causing trouble at England games.

I was given a 3 year civil banning order from inside every football ground in England and I was the first person in Nottinghamshire to receive one, but if I wanted to I could still go right up to the turnstiles, as I had no radius restrictions imposed on me.

Just before my ban I was shown on T.V. in an undercover programme about football hooliganism. I knew that they were filming a bit about Forest because at London Bridge they had a film crew outside the pub we were in and I asked a copper what was with the film crew. He said that the T.V. company were doing a documentary on Millwall but us lot had turned up and we'd stolen their thunder and took the shine away from them, so they'd decided to film us lot instead. It turned out to be total bollocks. On the night, it was shown on national T.V. I was at home lying on my bed, and it turned out that the programme had been filmed by some undercover reporter, and silly bollocks here was named and shamed. I nearly fell off my bed with the shock. I couldn't believe it. My mate Tommo phoned me and said that when it came on he was at home drinking a cup of tea and he nearly choked as he spat out his tea. He couldn't believe it. My phone never stopped ringing until about 2 in the morning with calls from all over the country. Luckily enough me mum and dad were abroad on holiday at the time but they later got to hear about it from their next-door neighbours. I'd been named and shamed.

bad and the ugly

Reporting team:
Leighton Kitson, Ruth
Shephard, Kevin Clark
and Patrick Lavelle.
Pictures: Peter Berry,
Kevin Brady and John
McCormick.

HUNDREDS of so-called English football fans and police officers clashed just minutes before the game kicked off, marring the carnival party atmosphere.

A massive security operation to head off any trouble had swung into place hours earlier, but as kick-off approached, mounted police officers, dog handlers and officers in riot gear moved in to control rising tempers among a core group of thugs intent on causing trouble.

A total of 93 people were arrested – none of them Turkish – throughout the evening as police moved to quell violence.

Although violence flared outside the Stadium of Light, many arrests were made following pockets of trouble in the city.

About 25 people – known Sunderland and Newcastle hooligans – were arrested near Boker Retail Park to prevent a

trouble — inadvertently trapping innocent bystanders and ticketholders. Several people

THE FACE OF SOCCER VIOLENCE : Above left, A suspect is restrained by a police dog and officers outside the Stadium of Light before the match. Right, a casualty of the violence.

Yob in jail for Euro 2004

By STEPHEN BEVAN

A VIOLENT Forest fan will spend Euro 2004 behind bars after pleading guilty to assaulting a Turkish fan before an England football game.

Gary Clarke, 38, from Arnold, was locked up following violence at last year's England v Turkey game in Sunderland.

Police in Nottingham say they are delighted with Clarke's imprisonment, and hope it will act as a deterrent to other soccer thugs who look up to him.

Trouble flared between rival supporters during the Euro 2004 qualifying match at the Stadium of Light last April.

Clarke, known by the police to be connected to the Forest Executive Crew hooligan gang, was caught by CCTV cameras attacking a rival fan before the game.

Newcastle Crown Court was told last week that Clarke went to the match without a ticket,

Gang leader admits attack on Turkey fan

and was seen kicking the Turkey supporter. Clarke required hospital treatment following the violence.

He was jailed for four months and banned from going to football grounds for six years after pleading guilty to affray.

Clarke had a similar ban imposed on him in 2001, which was due to run out later this year.

The court heard how he was part of a large group that had gathered near the ground when violence broke out.

Jamie Adams, in mitigation, said Clarke had been injured in the clash, resulting in him having nine stitches in his chest.

Notts Police Inspector Greg Drozdowski, of Police and Clubs Together, said because of Clarke's profile, the conviction was particularly rewarding: "It's a real boost for us in stamping out football violence not only nationally but internationally.

"Gary Clarke is considered a very high-profile member of the Forest Executive Crew hooligans and a lot of the other hooligans looked up to him.

"His conviction is a big coup for Notts Police especially before the Euro 2004 tournament.

"The ban now takes him out of the frame for the World Cup in 2006 and the following Euro championships in 2008."

Operation stops derby violence

Police swoop on hooligans

By STEVIE RODEN

INFORMATION: Insp Mark Holland

KNOWN hooligans were arrested in a police oper ation to crack down on violence during yesterday's Division One clash between Nottingham Forest and Derby County.

Police received information that rival gangs were to clash on the outskirts of Derby ahead of the sell-out game at Pride Park.

The Derby troublemakers never turned up for the anticipated showdown but scores of known Forest hooligans descended on Ilkeston to watch the game on television.

Police officers had to move in at the Ilkeston Social Club after fighting broke out towards the end of the match.

Bottles were thrown at officers and many of the troublemakers refused to disperse, leading to 27 arrests for public order offences and breach of the peace. Meanwhile, three Forest fans and five Derby supporters were arrested inside Pride Park for violent conduct offences.

Derbyshire police took the decision to arrest the people in Ilkeston for breach of the peace to stop the trouble spilling into the town centre or the centre of Derby later in the evening.

Inspector Mark Holland, of Notts police, travelled with police "spotters" to support the Derbyshire police-led operation.

He said: "A few of these troublemakers in Ilkeston had tickets for the game but never intended to get there. Their motives were to simply engage in fights.

"We knew where the hooligans would be and we managed to keep them all in one place.

"The arrests were made in the interest of public safety and helped make sure they could not engage in further trouble later in the day."

Derbyshire police brought the three Forest supporters arrested for violent conduct at Pride Park stadium back to Nottingham.

Arrests near hospital

FOUR people were arrested after trouble involving football supporters closed a road outside a hospital for more than an hour.

Part of the main road leading into the King's Mill Centre hospital at Sutton-in-Ashfield was closed on Saturday afternoon after Notts police reported a problem with a coach load of Huddersfield Town supporters before the start of the Field Mill match, which saw the visitors beat Mansfield Town 2-0.

Public bus and coach services were diverted away from the area. Four people were arrested for public disorder offences and the rest of the coach's occupants searched for offensive weapons before being escorted out of the county by police.

A spokeswoman for the hospital said: "Ambulances were still allowed through so it didn't cause any delay in the treatment of seriously injured patients. But patients coming into accident and emergency themselves reported that they had been stuck in traffic for a long time."

Lancashire Constabulary

<u>OPERATION FIXTURE</u>

DEAR SIR,

FOLOWING THE TRAGIC EVENTS OF THE 7th AND 8th OF DECEMBER 2002 WHHEN NATHAN SHAW WAS ASSAULTED AND DIED IN LANCASHIRE, YOU MAY BE AWARE THAT NATHANS FUNERAL IS TO TAKE PLACE ON FRIDAY 10th JANUARY 2003.ON SATURDAY THE 11th JANUARY 2003 NOTTINGHAM F.C. ARE PLAYING PRESTON NORTH END F.C. AT PRESTON.

AS A RESULT OF OUR INTELLIGENCE GATHERING OPERATIONS WE ARE AWARE THAT THERE ARE CERTAIN INDIVIDUALS THAT ARE INTENDING TO TRAVEL TO BURNLEY WITH THE INTENTION OF CAUSING DISORDER.

<u>IF YOU WERE CONSIDERING SUCH ACTION THEN TOGETHER WITH NATHANS FAMILY AND BOTH FOOTBALL CLUBS WE ARE ASKING THAT YOU DO NOT.</u>

IF YOU SHOULD CHOOSE TO IGNORE THE WISHES OF THE FAMILY AND ADVICE OF THE POLICE BE AWARE THAT THROUGHOUT THE WEEKEND OF THE 10th TO 12th JANUARY THERE WILL BE AN EXTENSIVE POLICING OPERATION ACROSS LANCASHIRE TO PREVENT DISORDER.THE OPERATION WILL INVOLVE BOTH LOCAL OFFICERS AND OFFICERS FROM NOTTINGHAM.

<u>DURING THIS WEEKEND YOUR MERE PRESENCE IN BURNLEY MAY RENDER YOU LIABLE TO ARREST AND ANY ATTEMPTS AT CAUSING DISORDER WILL BE RIGOROUSLY INVESTIGATED AND PROSECUTED</u>

CHAPTER 10

Champagne and Kebabs

J UST BEFORE I got my ban, England played Greece in a World Cup qualifier up at Old Trafford, and so I took a girlfriend along with me. I think she was enjoying herself but with England 2-1 down and with injury time disappearing fast, it didn't look good so we got up from our seats and made our way up the gangway towards the exit. Just as we were climbing the concrete steps, England were awarded a free kick and old Golden Balls Beckham stepped up to take it, he bent and swerved the ball past the Greek keeper and into the top corner of the net. Gooooooaaaaaaallll!! roared the crowd as we went fucking mental for a few seconds. I'd completely lost my girlfriend in all the celebrations and then I saw her a few steps below me. The Greek section of the crowd was silent and stood like showroom dummies. I bet not many of them had actually travelled from Greece and most of them looked like kebab shop owners from London. I'd had a chat with one of them before the game who had his daughter Donna with him.

That night when I got back into Nottingham I went to my local Greek restaurant, The Dioniss, in Arnold, and bought the owners and all the waiters a bottle of champagne to celebrate England qualifying for the World Cup in Japan, and the Greeks for playing so well and getting a well deserved draw. I had no hope in hell of getting out to Japan for the finals but in my mind I worked out a great route to beat the Old Bill and the Japanese authorities in getting into Japan. I planned to go out there if we got through to the semi final stages and I most definitely would have gone if we had of got through to the final. How could any football fan, banned or not, miss England in a World Cup final? Me and me mate Bergus, who's not a thug but loves his football and speaks dead posh, planned to fly to Moscow and then catch the Trans Siberian Express through Russia, Mongolia, and China and get a boat across to Japan. Clever eh? Whether it would have worked who knows?

When I got my ban, I still carried on going to the matches with the lads. We had Wolves away and about 80 of the lads met up in a pub in Clifton, which is on the outskirts of Nottingham. I hadn't plan on going but after a few beers I said "fuck it," so we drove over to Wolverhampton and got into this Indian-run pub, which is just around the corner from Molineux, at about 1.30 in the afternoon. Wolves were expecting us because Gilly, their main boy, had got my mobile number from me mate, Barry, from Northampton, who both me and Gilly knew from England games. I stayed in the pub with a couple of mates and the rest of them set off for the game. A lot of them had stolen tickets as the ticket office at Molineux had been recently broken into and some of the stolen tickets had found their way into some of our boys' hands. As they went to go into the ground the Old Bill broke up a bit of a scuffle near the turnstiles, they then checked our boys' tickets and nicked about 15 of them on the spot for the stolen tickets. I didn't get involved and when I heard what had happened, I fucked off. If Wolves had of come to the pub looking for a row, I'd have had it, but I wasn't going looking for it. I'm not that daft.

Around this time, I also started going to a few Newcastle games and enjoyed their boys' company. It's always a good night out up there and I wasn't so well known by the Police. I also went with our lot to West Ham away. 250 of us got the service train from Nottingham to London. We hadn't played West Ham for a few years and some of our, young'ens had never been there. Also, Derby were playing in London on the same day so the potential for fireworks was there. They were playing Brentford in the F.A. Cup but it turns out they only took 30 lads so they shit out again. In addition, Middlesbrough, were at Chelsea that day. We stayed in the Blind Beggar pub over in the east end of London. The rest of the lads got over to the game about 10 minutes before kick off, and waiting for them was 50 to 60 West Ham standing outside the Queens pub.

"What time do ya call this?" said a few of them, pointing to the time on their watches. After the game we filled a pub up at Victoria and word had it was that Boro were coming over for a row. We'd been chatting to half a dozen of them that morning in a pub near to Kings Cross Station. No one touched them but we let them know what our plans were for later. We waited for a couple of hours and there was no sign of Boro or any other mob, coming to us for a row. We had a massive mob and some began to get restless. Some wanted action and drifted off north and back up towards Kings Cross. We couldn't move off as one because of our huge numbers, so we jumped into taxis and headed towards Kings Cross station. As our cab pulled up after the drive across London, we saw coming towards us a football mob and it turned out to be Boro, but they had Old Bill all around them. I walked straight in amongst them and gave a few of them a shoulder barge and the odd sly elbow in the guts and ribs.

"Come on Boro" I said out of the corner of my mouth, but not wanting to draw the Old Bill's attentions to me. But none of them wanted to know. "Boatsy," I heard one of them shout, and coming towards me with his hand outstretched, was one of their lads, Craig, who I know well. We exchanged pleasantries and then the Old Bill rounded us up with the rest of the Forest lads that they were holding outside McDonald's restaurant. We were held there for an hour on the pavement while the Old Bill escorted Derby County's' 20-strong, tin-pot army onto their train home.

At about 8 o'clock, we were put on a Nottingham-bound train, escorted all the way by the police. All was peaceful until someone pulled the train's communication cord and we tried to get off at Leicester but the Old Bill was having none of it. We took five thousand fans to Upton Park for that game and to tell you the truth the lads were quite disappointed by the size of the waiting I.C.F. welcoming committee. Although a few words were exchanged, nothing else happened. I think some of the youngsters thought we'd been lying to them all these years with the stories of just how tough it was at West Ham. I'm only joking! On their day West Ham were a top firm but I think them days are gone. Same with most of us.

Another day out I had with our lads and the Newcastle lads was the England v Finland game in a World Cup qualifier up at Liverpool. A few took a bus and about 30 of us caught the service train up there and got off at Lime Street, where we all met up in a back-street pub. Most of the lads went into the game but four others and me stayed in the pub and watched the game on the telly. We'd met a fair sized Huddersfield mob in Manchester on the way up and there were mobs of geezers from other teams roaming about all over the place. There was me and Mr. Handsome Palmer, and three Geordie lads sitting drinking and engrossed in the game. Out of the corner of my eye, I noticed a group of lads had come to the door and I knew by their body language that they weren't coming in to say hello and have a drink. My first impressions told me they were here for trouble and I was dead right as they burst in, I picked up a stool and went towards the door. As I looked around to see who was behind me I noticed Palmer leaning over the bar kissing the barmaid, and then a bottle whizzed past my head, just missing me. Punches were thrown so I threw the stool at them and they backed off, I some how managed to get the door shut, and took a deep breath the adrenalin was pumping, through the frosted glass of the pub windows I could see them going to the other end of the pub where there was another entrance. The landlord moved a bit rapid got there before they could get in and he locked the door. As this was happening a cab pulled up outside and Johnny King and Little Scotty and a couple of our other lads, stepped onto the pavement and this mob stuck outside, attacked them and were battering the fuck out of them. We got the pub door open and came steaming out, with stools and bottles and they hesitated and spread out in the road.

"You're Forest," said one of them.

"That's right," I replied, holding a stool ready for more action.

Someone on their side threw a punch and it kicked- off again but as soon as it started the Old Bill turned up in force and put a stop to it. I had a bit of problem though because when they first attacked the pub a cunt with them threw a glass at me and it hit me in the face gashing my nose which had been pissing blood I was covered in claret and the coppers were most interested in me, and how I'd got in such a state. My adrenalin had been pumping that much I'd forgot all about it, as you do in situations like that. The landlord came out, backed us up, and told the coppers we were the victims and had been no trouble all the time that we'd been in his pub. The Old Bill came back into the pub with us and told us to keep a low one for the rest of the day. I went into the toilets and cleaned myself up. It turns out that the mob we'd been fighting with were an Aston Villa and Sunderland firm that had joined up together to attack us. Villa's main lad, Fowler, was there, but why he'd want to join up with them Mackem cunts puzzles me. We then walked down to the Crown pub and by now, most of our lads were on their way back from the match, so now there's, more of us. We walk in the pub and it's full of Mackems. One of the Newcastle lads cracks this Mackem on the jaw and it's all off as tables and chairs go flying. The Old Bill turn up and grab me, and Palmer and handcuff us to the railings outside the pub.

"Right Clarke," says the Old Bill who obviously knew me.

"I have now seen you involved in two incidents".

I'm thinking "this is it, I'm nicked," but to my amazement he sends us on our way with just a warning.

"If I see you again you're nicked".

And I did see him again. Not that night but about a year later when he came to give evidence against me in court when I got my civil banning order. He gave this story as part of his evidence against me.

That night there was running battles all over the city centre between rival gangs of England firms. Later on Everton had a big mob out and by all accounts they were doing the business.

We left town when the Geordies boarded their bus for home and so it was time for us to go. It just shows what bully cunts them Villa and Mackem cunts are. I remember a few years back when Mansfield played Sunderland in a pre-season friendly. Forest and Mansfield combined and turned out a 150 strong mob and a few of me Geordie mates came down to have a go at the Mackem slags, who were on the phone to us all day long telling us that they were coming and what they were going to do. We were waiting and watching for them in Mansfield when we got a call, while the game was going on, telling us that they are drinking in Nottingham in a bar down by the canal side. It turns out they're with their Villa mates so we jumped into a fleet of cabs with the coppers in hot pursuit, following us in their cars. Before we could get near them the Old Bill had realized what was going to happen and had them surround, they then turned their attentions on us and told us that they've been watching us all day long and why was we in Mansfield one minute and then dashing back to Nottingham the next? A fucking stupid question, they pushed us back up the road, and escorted them out of the city. Since then the Villa and Sunderland connection still remains a mystery to us all.

Derby away was another game where I was arrested, yet again, 150 of us met at Eastwood Town's football ground and were drinking in the club house. We'd been speaking to some of their boys about the game and we told them we wouldn't be coming into their town centre because it was all cameras and C.C.T.V. We told them a fair few of our boys were on these banning orders, and a lot of their lads were also banned, so we said 'O. K.' why not move the venue for some action. Their football copper was one England's main spotter's so he took a few of them lot out first with these bans, not because they had a bigger hooligan problem then anyone else, but he simply started on his own club first as he could sort out the Derby faces that went to England games. It was as simple as that. So the Derby lot saw sense and called it on for a meet in Ilkeston, which is between Derby and Nottingham, but then they cancelled that meet because a landlord in a pub had got wind of what was about to happen and told the police. They then wanted us to go into Derby. "Fuck it," we all said, "let's go to Ilkeston". We set off in our cars but as soon as we pulled out of the car park the Old Bill were waiting and had sealed off the road and were pulling everyone over, we were ordered out of the cars and then searched while a police video camera was stuffed in your face. All this was going on while a police helicopter hovered overhead. Apparently, there was a rumor that the Nottingham Old Bill had followed me from my house, that morning but to tell you the truth I never noticed them. Just look at the money they waste. If I was a sex offender I'd have more rights. I'd be allowed outside a school's gates. It's a fucking joke, do the public know how much money is wasted? Some people might say "but your, a football hooligan and you should know what to expect from the police", the answer to that is "I do know, but it's so over the top". Who gives authorization to waste so much money on such a small problem? People who fight at football only fight like-minded people, true or False? I'll tell you its true and that's a fact take it from me.

This game was a Sunday fixture and one of our lads from Eastwood had arranged for the club bar to be open at 9 o'clock in the morning. When we pulled in at the car park, there was no sign of any coppers. It wasn't until about an hour later when the helicopter came hovering overhead that we knew something was up. What must the good people of Eastwood think about being woken up at such an ungodly hour by those boys in blue buzzing their rooftops? Is there no consideration for the decent people left in this world? Once we were processed by the Old Bill the minivan I was in was allowed to go on its way.

We stopped in a pub in another part of Eastwood for a while and then drove over to Ilkeston. As soon as I stepped from the mini bus I was traveling in, the Old Bill grabbed me and I was arrested. I was put in a police van and taken to Derby's main police station. There's police stations nearer so where was the sense in that? Seven of us in total were nicked and taken away and were held until five o'clock and then released without charge into Derby town centre. The game was a 1 o'clock kick-off so by the time we came out the game had been over a couple of hours. When I was first arrested I must admit I was a bit worried and thought it was a bit of a set-up and that a certain copper could make life very difficult for me. When I was in police custody, I had visions of getting, properly filled in and I told our copper, Smiler, my feelings at the time of my arrest.
"Don't worry Gary" he said, "we wouldn't let that happen," and to tell you the truth the Derby Old Bill never said a word to us all the time I was in there. Thinking back over it, this was another Derby no show but then again, what's new?

CHAPTER 11

Fame at Last?

ENGLAND V TURKEY in a European championship qualifier was a recipe for trouble. Two Leeds fans had been stabbed to death on the streets of Istanbul prior to a Leeds utd European game and anti-Turkish feeling was running high, plus every time a British team played out in Turkey there would be scenes of chaos at the airport and the threat of violence towards the visiting teams and their supporters. Banners and placards with "Welcome to Hell" written on them, and players and fans being spat at, seemed to be the norm, and attacks by Turkish fans and their police were shown on British T. V. and were reported in the press and media. An old aged pensioner following Man Utd had been attacked and taken from his hotel room. Even Eric Cantona had been attacked by Turkish police as he left the field of play at the end of a game. What had the football authorities done about these and other incidents? I'll tell you what they done. Fuck all, that's what they did. So the word on the street was that groups of England fans would be out for revenge.

The game was to be held at Sunderland's Stadium of Light and was taking place on a Wednesday evening. Me and Lenny took a couple of days off work and travelled up on the Tuesday to watch the England under 21s play against Turkey at Newcastle's St. James Park. We watched the game in a bar with a few of my Geordie mates and a couple of West Ham lads tagged along, and one of them turned out to be Bonzo who I've known for years through the England scene. So we had a good night on the piss. I'd first met Bonzo in Germany in'88 and it was a number of years since I'd seen him. He's a top bloke and well liked by the rest of the England lads.

The following morning I met up with the Geordie lads, who had a pub sorted near the Tyne tunnel, then the Forest and Mansfield lads began turning up in cars and mini buses. By four o'clock, there must have been

150 of us. We took the Metro to Seaburn, which is in an area of Sunderland, and is about a 20-minute journey, from Newcastle. We didn't have a single copper with us as we got off and we made our way out onto the street and towards 'The Four Bells' pub. There was only a few Mackems in there but they were soon on their toes as a stool went crashing behind the bar and the windows were smashed in. The Geordies were well up for it and just wanted to have it with Sunderland's firm. We maneuvered around the back streets and roads avoiding the Old Bill until we came to 'The Wheatsheaf' pub where we knew the bulk of the Mackem mob would be drinking. The thing was we'd come in from the direction of the seafront, which put the coppers and the Mackems off, of our scent. The rest of the England lads were in the town centre and we'd heard that Leeds and Boro both had big mobs out on that day. Most of the Old Bill was busy keeping order in town so we'd arrived relatively undetected. The 'Wheatsheaf' is on a stretch of road, which is known locally as 'The Gauntlet', and it has half a dozen other pubs nearby to it. Every pub around there that night was packed solid and as we approached 'The Wheatsheaf' a mob on seeing us approaching come out and move towards us. They know we've arrived but they didn't know who we were. A police helicopter appeared and hovered overhead. We got near enough almost right on top of the pub and it went fucking ballistic. Bottles and glasses were thrown at us and they had the numbers but we were going nowhere, and as we moved towards them, they backed off. "They've here they've hear" you could hear a Mackem voice scream. A few of them were caught and put on their arses. The Old Bill came flying in with truncheons drawn and got in between the two mobs. We moved back off up the road we'd just come down from when a mob of Sunderland came out on to a small industrial estate from a side alley, it was just as my Forest mate Dave, appeared in his car. I had just spoken to him on the phone about tickets for the match. He'd driven from Newcastle and kept in touch with us by mobile phone. He was the one that guided us into town, telling us what to avoid and what Metro station to get off at, there was about 40 Sunderland that came bouncing out in front of us half a dozen Forest lads, the rest of the Geordies had moved off, and hadn't seen this Mackem mob. A few of them were carrying what looked like piece's of wooden pallet. I walked towards one of them and he swung a lump of this wood at me, and it broke on my arm.

"Come on if you want it," I shouted, and the lot of them ran off.

Next thing, I've got someone hanging on my back, "Fuck off," I shout trying to shrug them off. I look around and it's a copper with a dog. He must have literally grabbed me seconds after the geezer's hit me with the wood, and because they'd run off and legged it, so all he's seen, is me bouncing around, he don't know the whole story so he grabs hold of me. I didn't know who the fuck he was as he's grabbed me from behind, the next minute the police dog comes from the side of me and jumps up and sinks its teeth into my upper arm. The dog handler wouldn't call the dog off or tell it to let go until I was down on the ground. I was in agony and he then called the dog off as I was lifted to my feet by a group of Old Bill and put in the back of a police van, a group of Newcastle Old Bill come over, and one says in broad Geordie accent.

"Hello Gary".

I just smiled.

"I'll tell you what," he said to his Sunderland colleagues, "wherever he is," pointing at me "the Newcastle Gremlins won't be far away".

"Great, fuck me, that's all I want to hear," I'm thinking.

I'm in fucking agony where the dog's fucking bit me on the arm, and I've also got, a right searing, burning pain in my chest.

When we get to the police station I'm in complete agony and can hardly talk with the pain, and I tell them I feel unwell. After a while, they listen to me and take me to a cell where I strip off down to my boxer shorts, and a police photographer comes in and takes photos of my injuries. I'm then taken to hospital in a police van with two of the best looking police women I've ever seen. They were fucking gorgeous. The nurse at the hospital inspects my wounds as I sit there handcuffed, watching the England game on the hospital T.V. I'm then taken down for x-rays and they take my handcuffs off. A few England fans come in and I recognize one of them from Mansfield. He'd also been bitten by a police dog on the leg. While I'm waiting for my x-rays I get chatting to these two W.P.C.s about the night life in Newcastle and I'm having a crack about me taking them out and where we should go for a drink when I get out of here and when they've next off duty. Then another copper comes along and 'as a word with them on the quiet and they come back in and tell me that their boss has told them to put the handcuffs back on me as I'm likely to run off. One of them does the handcuffs back up and I place my coat over them to hide them. I'm x-rayed and it turns out the wound on my chest is not a dog bite but a stab wound. There was no blood, just an open wound, and you could see the tissue inside. I had ten stitches and was cleaned up and injected and while all this was happening, I had a copper standing over me, watching. An older copper just being nosey comes into where I'm being treated and takes a look at my wound he shakes his head and mumbles, "I knew someone would get stabbed tonight". As I laid there, I cast my mind back to just before I got nicked and I tried to remember seeing someone with a knife. But the only thing that might have happened was that the lump of wood that the Mackem was swinging around could have had a nail in it and because my adrenalin was pumping, I didn't feel it go into me. But whatever it was that went into my chest, it tore me open as clean as a whistle. I was in the hospital for 6 hours getting treatment and then I was taken back to the police station to be interviewed by the local C.I.D. The hospital nearly kept me in over night and back at the police station I gave my account of what had happened, and around 2.30 a.m. they let me go on bail. I pointed out to them that all the nightclubs would be turning out around this time and I would be taking my life in my hands walking the streets of Sunderland at that hour of the night. One of the coppers, who was a half decent bloke, told me he was finished work now and that he would drop me off at a taxi rank. They just done the interview with me, and gave me no grief whatsoever.

The first taxi rank that we came to was full of lads and many of them were dressed in Stone Island gear, which more or less meant they were football lads. "I aint getting out here," I protested.
The copper laughed and told me I was spot on as the lads in the taxi queue were some of Sunderland's Seaburn Casuals. We followed a taxi up the road and as the cabbie pulled over to drop off his fare the copper got out, and approached the driver and flashed his warrant card. He explained that I needed a taxi back to Newcastle and the cabbie agreed to take me I shook hands with the copper and I went off in the back of the taxi. I got the cab to me mate Skeenys, who was from Nottingham but was now living in Newcastle. I paid the cab driver the £20 fare and slept the night at Skeenys.

The next morning my boss from work was on the phone asking me where I was and why wasn't I at work and that I should go out immediately and buy that mornings papers. I didn't have to ask, I just knew. I stayed put on Skeeny's settee while he went out and got the papers. When he came back, he laid them out in front of me and I knew then I was in some serious shit. They must have taken these photos of me being bitten and apprehended by the copper with the dog, from a passing car or something. How the fuck they got those photos I'll never know. I also appeared on Sky News, which goes worldwide. I was fucked. I was infamous at last. My mind and head was swimming and spinning and I had a hundred million things going around inside it. I phoned my mum and dad, and told them that I was all right, and that I was not as badly hurt as they might have heard. I spent another day at Skeeny's just keeping a low one and then I went home, but they didn't want to talk about it. They were disgusted by it all. I was all bandaged up and went off to my local to have a couple of pints at lunchtime, and in there is one of the Forest football spotters.

"Had a spot of bother up north then mate?" he laughed.

"It looks like it," I said, and he walked off laughing and shaking his head.

I had a week off work and wherever I went people would stare and nudge one another. Maybe they thought I was Robbie Williams or somebody famous. One of our young lads, Adam, who goes to football with me, opened up the paper at work the morning after and nearly fell off the chair in the canteen as he saw me with the police dog hanging off me. When I got back to work, did I get some stick off the blokes? It was never ending.

I went to see my solicitor, who I'd used since I was young, and he'd always tried his best for me, and in the past had got me, out of some right scrapes. He advised me to plead not guilty and thought I had a good case. I went up to Sunderland magistrates where people who were going up before the judge were getting let off with fines. I pleaded not guilty to the original charge of threatening behaviour and I kept getting put off and told to come back at a later date. All in all I went back five times, on my next visit a mate of mine, Trev from Nottingham, was up on the same charge as me and plus they had film of him actually punching somebody. He copped a £250 fine and no ban. I was thinking "fucking hell, I should have gone guilty and had it all over and done with," but it got worse as the Old Bill upped my charge to affray. I couldn't believe it. Part of their evidence against me was my old mate from the Derbyshire constabulary following me around on the night and filming me, out of 150 strong mob he concentrated on me I think someone had it in for me and now I'm worried. I'd also not heard from my solicitor for weeks before the trial so from him being dead confident for months and months there was now nothing but silence and, I was the one now having to chase him. Something was odd with the whole thing.

Fifteen months later it eventually goes to trial and with all the evidence stacked against me I'm willing to change my plea to guilty for the threatening behaviour if they drop the affray charge. I'm bollocked as they have me on film but it's not in the proper sequence. The bit when I'm attacked by the Mackem with the plank of wood has been taken out. The video shown in court is not the original one that I'd seen at my solicitors. Bits are missing and things just don't add up. The whole thing stinks. The pub fight is shown after I'm hit with the wood. The film is not in the proper sequence at all. The barrister I had defending me was told of this but didn't really take up the point. The case lasted a day at Newcastle Crown Court and I plead guilty, and then my previous is read out and I know I'm well and truly fucked. The judge passes a 4 month custodial sentence with the words of the prosecution ringing in my ears about being a menace to society and that I'm the leader of this and the ring leader of that. It was the week before Euro 2004 in Portugal started and I feel I was being made a bit of a scapegoat. I had become a thorn in someone's side and to this day, I have never heard from my solicitor, someone I'd known for over 20 years. Does that tell you something?

CHAPTER 12 # A Rest to Make Plans

FTER MY sentencing I still had the words of the judge swimming around in my head, who basically said that someone of my age and standing should know better and not get involved in this sort of thing. He'd also given me on top of my 4 month prison sentence, a 6 year banning order, which included a ten mile radius ban whenever Nottingham Forest were playing away, a one mile radius ban from the stadium, when Forest were playing at home and plus the ban covered England games and Newcastle games at home and in Europe. I was to also hand my passport into my local police station five days before a match and to cover these games. This ban covered every football stadium in England and Wales and I knew in my heart before I was sentenced that I was going to go away, but I'd had good support in court from my friends who were all there when I was sent down. I had a girlfriend from Newcastle for the last 3 months and she came down to the cells to say goodbye. I was gutted. The following week I was due to fly off to Thailand for a holiday on my birthday.

I hadn't told my mum and dad anything about this case as they were getting on a bit and I didn't want to put them through the worry of it all. If I'd have got off with it and walked free they would have been none the wiser, but the problem was that the plan was that if I did get put away then my sister was to tell them of my predicament. However, she'd gone away to the Lake District and no one could get hold of her because she had no signal on her mobile phone. I used to go around every Monday or Tuesday with my dirty washing for mum to sort out and when I didn't show up it was left to my sister, who had now heard the news, to tell them that I was on a little vacation.

I was taken off to Durham prison to start my sentence and when we got there I was surprised at just how old the place was. It's an old, Victorian, crumbling jail, like something off an old 40s or 50s black and white British gangster film. You look up and you can see all the landings with the safety nets and the drab, grey, green painted walls and the heavy cell doors with a spy hole cut in. The smell and noise hits you straight away. Cooked cabbage, piss and disinfectant attack your nostrils. I got in there about 3 o'clock in the afternoon and it took about an hour to go through all the checking in procedure You're first placed in a reception room with all the other people who've come in on your wagon that day. I'm suited and booted and the others are dossers and tramps, which are dressed well like tramps. Most by the sounds of it have been in before and it seemed they were forever in and out of the place for petty crimes, as most of the screws know them. I was the only person there with a different accent and I had to really listen to what was being said to me. It was like I was in another country and I was struggling with the language. Your name is called and you tell the screw what you're in for, and then you're told to sit down and wait. After a while, you're told to strip off and the clothes you've come in are folded up and put into a cardboard box, which is taken away from you, and you're then handed a pile of prison clothes to wear. I was given a pair of jeans, a couple of white plain tee shirts some striped prison shirts and a pair of plain black leather shoes. I was then taken to the reception wing where I was met by a few cons that work there, welcoming, if that's the right word, the new cons. I had a chat with them, and I told them what I was in for and we talk about football and everything's fine.

The first night I'm in there I'm sharing a cell with a half-caste lad from Sunderland. I don't believe it. I can't get away from Mackems. He was all right, as it happened and he showed me the ropes. He then asked if I minded if he had a Derby County (a shit). I said, "be my guest." Most cells had their own toilets so there was no slopping out. He had a dump and then went down on his hands and knees and fished through the cable he'd just laid in the toilet and pulled out a lump of Moroccan black, wrapped in cellophane, which he said he swallowed just before going to court. I spent the first night watching him getting stoned out of his nut. I'd already had a pull by the prison doctor when I was drug tested in reception and I proved positive for both cocaine and puff. The night before I went to court me mate had a bong we were all puffing on back at my hotel, and I also had a couple of lines of Charlie to relax me before the trial. The doctor gave me a funny look and asked me routine questions about drugs and if I had any sort of habit. I gave him a load of bollocks about being nervous about the trial and he accepted all my explanations. A week later I was tested again and nothing was found in my system and all tests proved negative.

The first night in there I sat and wrote a letter to my dad telling him how sorry I was about what I'd put them through and that I would be fine and would see them soon. To this day, the old man has never ever mentioned that letter. The following day I got some money together and got a phone card and used the pay phone on the landing to phone home. The conversation was strained to say the least, but it was good to hear mum and dad's voices. If I had any chance of getting out of here early on a tag I needed to stay clean and drug free. If you got caught smoking dope by one of the screws then they'd nick you and you'd go on report and lose remission. The Mackem I was banged up with knew when to smoke and when not to smoke. He knew the system inside out and had been in and out of various prisons for the last 10 years, and was an experienced con.

I was banged up 23 hours a day and the only time you were allowed from your cell was to get your food, and then it was straight back in and banged up again. You'd get one-hour association when you could play pool or use your phone card. I just used to sit down and chill out and try to gather my thoughts, plus it was nice to get away from Bob Marley and his spliffs and breathe some fresh air. One of the screws used to come over and have a chat with me and the talk got around to football and his team were Newcastle United, which was no surprise as I was in Durham nick. It turned out he knew a few of the lads from The Adelphi Hotel and had even been to Newcastle games I'd been at.

One day he came to my cell with a sheet of paper which he said basically stated that I had worked all my life and that on it he had added that he had got to know me and that I was a good lad.

"Sign this," he said, "and I'll sort you out a decent job within the prison."
"It will be good pay and will get you out of your cell."

But before I could start my new career I was moved to another wing and this new place was a bit more nerve racking, the bloke opposite me was doing life. The reason I knew this was on the front of the cell doors was a little card, mine had "4 months" written on it and the bloke across the landing had "life" written on his, which was somewhat worrying. He was a big muscleman who thought he was Jack the Biscuit but was a right twat, but at the time, I found it best not to mention it to him.

During association people would go to him to have their hair shaved, and one day I was queuing and his mates were turning up and were pushing in and having theirs done ahead of me and he could see this happening but said nothing. He loved winding people up. I walked off and went back to my cell in a huff.

"Don't worry about it," said my cellmate. "He's doing it to wind you up."
"Don't worry about it, he's doing life and you're doing 4 months so who's the cunt?"

He was one horrible cunt who'd goad anyone into a fight so they'd get into trouble when they got caught they'd then end up having to do a longer sentence. He was the one that had nothing to lose and he knew that. I went up to him and said that if he cut my hair then I'd give him a few men's mags like 'Front' or 'F.H.M.' as I was being well looked after with gear being sent in by mates on the outside. So I ended up giving him the magazines and he cut my hair and he was all right about that. Another time I had a black lad from France cut it. He was half African and half French. I remember when France were playing and he was listening on the radio and the French scored. He went fucking mad. He was two cells down from me yet I could still hear him. He once tried to flog me some diamonds, which he said he could get his hands on. I told him that once I got out I'd look him up and try to shift some for him. What else could I say? A lot of people kept themselves to themselves and to be honest I didn't speak to a lot of people. Most people I spoke to thought I was from London with my accent.

The job I'd got in reception didn't happen and when I tried to get a job as a trustee with a red band, which meant I could work in the gardens, there was a bit of an outcry so I had to wait for a decent job. The last time I saw the screw that followed Newcastle I shook his hand and told him that if I ever saw him out in Newcastle then I would buy him a pint. He was a decent bloke.

I thought I'd spend my entire sentence in Durham and I was offered a job in the laundry and the screw in there knew who I was as he'd heard all about me and knew all my Gremlin mates from Newcastle. When I arrived in the laundry the work came to a standstill as cons gathered around to speak to me about football. I was like a film star holding court.

"We've had all the Gremlins in here," said the screw, reeling their names off, so proud that he'd met them. He'd find any excuse to come and chat to me. The good thing about the laundry was you got to get an hour and a half for your dinner, but it was still the same prison grub which was fucking shit. It was disgusting. It was served on a metal tray with your normally stone-cold dinner slopped on it, with a revolting pudding fermenting next to it. It was pure pigswill.

One morning a woman prison worker came down to see me and told me I'd got a chance to move to Wealstun prison, which is near Wetherby. I told her I was happy to be in Durham because my mates from Newcastle, and my local girlfriend, found it easy to visit me. She went on to say that if I moved, there was a better chance of home leaves and that I could get tagged earlier and plus have more freedom down there. She left me thinking about it but said she advised me to take it. I chatted about it with my cellmate who said I'd be silly not to take it. He'd heard it was like a holiday camp down there. I'd been in Durham 13 days and in a funny way I'd got used to life in there, even though it was grim, and I'd got to know the screws and the way things worked. Anyway, I agreed to move on and the next morning at 7.00, I was on my way out, with about eight others, in the back of a prison van.

When we got down there we couldn't believe it. It was set in the middle of the Yorkshire countryside and there were two prisons. One was a category D and one was a category C, and there was people just walking around unsupervised. As soon as I got into the reception, I was handed some clothes that my girlfriend, Claire, had bought into Durham for me but I wasn't allowed to wear. She'd sent in my own pair of trainers and some Armani jeans and tee shirts. I put them straight on and felt a million dollars, and was half way back to being a normal person. The whole system was dead relaxed in there, but the one drawback was I was banged up with another Mackem, but this cunt did my head in. His fucking feet stank and he was a right scruffy cunt, who never seemed to shower or wash. One of the lads who came down with me from Durham went on an education course but because I wasn't due to stay in there that long they wouldn't let me go on one. All they offered me was a job in the laundry but I didn't fancy washing other cons' socks and pants so luckily they put me on a computer course. One of the boys, I'd just come down from Durham with came down to the classroom to see how I was getting on and to tell me there were three Leeds lads that had got nicked at the England v Turkey game, in there.

That night two Leeds lads came down to my cell to see me, I had one on my own now as I'd got rid of the smelly Mackem. They told me that they could get me anything I wanted their mates would come past the perimeter fence and throw bottles of booze over for them. They were both in for 18 months for fighting with some Turks at the game. I'd followed them through the prison system. They'd met some Turks in a car park near the ground and had a vicious fight with them and the Turks were well tooled up, but the three Leeds lads stood their ground and it was they that were arrested and sent down.

All in all I served 31 days, doing 13 of them in Durham. It was an experience, a bit of a rest really. At night, we'd walk around the football field and we weren't back in our cells until 10 o'clock, plus you could get any drink or drug that took your fancy. I wasn't to sure when I was going to be released but three days before I was due out a probation officer came to see me and told me I was being released on a tag and that I'd have to have a permanent address to go to. Which I did have.

I was released, at about 7.30 in the morning, and me mates Harry and Steve, from Nottingham, came to pick me up. We stopped off and had breakfast on the way home and when we arrived back in Nottingham, at about 10.30, I went in the pub initially to just have a couple of pints of Guinness. All day long people were popping in and out of the pub to have a drink and to see me, and time just flew by, so dead on 3 o'clock I was running through the streets of Arnold to get home to have the tag fitted to my ankle. I was shitting myself that I'd missed them but they didn't turn up until 7 p.m. They fitted it and it felt a bit uncomfortable, the electronic tag works on the idea that you're allowed to leave your home between the hours of 7 a.m. and 7.15 p.m. for work purposes. The rest of the time you are supposed to be indoors, at home. A signal is sent from the tag to the monitoring centre giving accurate details of where you are at any given time. If you break the rules of being tagged you go straight back to prison to finish your sentence.

On my first day back at work I got a call from me mate who lives with me, telling me the tag monitoring people had been on the phone asking why I was out of the house at 6.40 a.m. My gaffer phoned the prison and sorted it out that I was allowed out of the house at 6.30 a.m. to set off for work and so the drama was sorted. In Prison I'd been laying on me arse and having a rest for the last 30 odd days so I was eager to get back to work. Prison was like a rest. I didn't mind it. I was the fittest I'd been for years and I'd been off the booze and everything else for over a month. I enjoyed it really and had a clean bill of health. I felt brand new.

The tag took a couple of days to get used to and at first it felt a bit uncomfortable but I soon forgot that I even had it on.

Dave White, my Rangers mate, outside Ibrox.

A few of the Forest lads on tour.

Top left: Most of our firm have Forest tattooed in their lips.

Bottom left: Fred and Johnny handsome.

Top right and below: Barcelona 2005.

Photo session with MK

ON TOUR WITH MK
BARCA 2005.

Top left: Len, Me and MK, Barca 2005.

Botton left: Kingy's yacht.

Top right: With my mate Spence from Oldham, in Thai.

The Greyhound Crew, July 2005.

Left: The Greyhound Crew, 2005.

Below: Me, Fred and Sukkiy.

Top right: A Saturday night in Nottingham.

Bottom Right: 'Hang on, I'm having my photo done.

Me and my good mate Lenny.

CHAPTER 13

The Good, The Bad and The Useless

AFTER MY first day back at work I went home, had a drink and was still full of energy and wasn't in the slightest bit tired so I lay down on my bed and let a thousand things wash over me and go through my mind. I thought of the holiday in Thailand I'd missed through going to prison. I thought about my time in prison, the losers in there, the people who adjust to the regime in there, the people who shouldn't be in there, and then I thought about why I'd been sent there and what it achieved or didn't achieve for me. I thought of all the boys out in Thailand drinking in the Dogs Bollocks bar, talking bollocks. I thought of Jeff, Chris and Barrels, who own it and run it. I thought of all the people I'd met through supporting Forest and following the England team, and then my mind and memory went back, in some cases to years gone by, and the friends I'd made and the faces and clubs, I'd battled with. Here are some of my thoughts and feelings on some of those teams and this is in no particular order.

Chelsea

I know a lot of the Chelsea lads and to me their mob has always been one of the best. Forest have been down there a few times and have always done reasonably well, but the first time I went there was in the early 80s with Leeds. 200 fans got arrested on the underground after battles with mobs of Chelsea. I was late getting down to London so I missed all the rows and it was a good job I did because old muggings here would have definitely got nicked. It was the season when all the Chelsea fans came on the pitch at the end of the game and ran towards the Leeds' fans behind the goal. Chelsea were well up for it and even the stewards at pitch side were offering the Leeds' fans out and goading them for a fight. It was mental. That day I was 16 or 17 at the time and stood there laughing my head off thinking "this Chelsea lot are crackers." I'd heard all the tales about Chelsea coming to Forest in the 70s and at one game when Chelsea's Ian Britton scored, there were several stabbings and that night the game was on 'Match of the Day'. That year Chelsea were given our end, The Trent End, and Chelsea fans to this day insist that they took the Trent End. I saw Chelsea at first hand when I watched them at Cambridge so I know what they're like. We've been down there a few times with a good mob but we've never really bumped into one another. We took a 200 strong mob down there one New Years Day, around '85 and we started off the day drinking in a few gay bars around Vauxhall. From there we caught the tube to Fulham Broadway, came out, walked up the road and tried to get in The Shed End. That day I was walking around with a walking stick making out to the Old Bill that I had a dodgy leg and was walking with a limp. I'd been out New Years Eve on the piss and to tell you the truth I was still half cut when I got up to go to the game. When my mate called around for me I grabbed my coat from the cupboard and saw my dad's walking stick, and on the spur of the moment I took it thinking I could have some fun with it. Plus at the time Chelsea had a right reputation so I thought it would come in handy. Outside the ground the Old Bill called a halt to our little expedition.

"Where are you going lads and what team are ya?" they asked.

We all played dumb and never answered.

"Make ya mind up lads."

Still no answer from us and with that they rounded us all up and stuck us in the away end, which in them days was in the North stand, which was a rambling, open end with cracked concrete steps and rusty looking safety barriers. A copper, on spotting me with a limp and a walking stick, even helped me up a particularly steep set of terracing, bless him!

Then again, in the mid 90s I ran two buses down there and we was at Earls Court at 11 o'clock in the morning. We don't go in the ground and we had a right good firm. We then moved on to an Irish bar on the Fulham Road and about 4 o'clock the Old Bill came in, shut the pub and told us we were out of there and was escorted out of London on the bus. I remember they walked us through a graveyard and slung us on the buses. On the way back up the M1 we stopped off in Leicester and attacked their main pub. We C.S. gassed about 30 to 40 of them in there and because of our numbers they wouldn't come out. I think Chelsea and Forest have a great respect for one another that goes back a long way. Martin King once told me that Mr. Chelsea, the legendary Micky Greenaway, who's no longer with us, told him that the original football mob were Nottingham Forest he'd been there with a small group of Chelsea fans in the early 60s and on leaving the train station, was attacked by a larger, very well organised mob of Forest fans. Not long after that he set about organising Chelsea's mob along the same lines and the Chelsea Shed was born, and the rest is history.

Last year I was in Barcelona and happened to be out there the same time as Chelsea were playing a Champions League game in Spain. In a back street bar I met Babs, who is a legend in Nottingham. We chatted about football and had a few beers and he also spoke highly about Forest's mob and had nothing but respect for our firm over the years. He turned out to be great company and the perfect gentleman, but then again I didn't expect him to be anything else. So you can see I've grown to have a bit of a soft spot for Chelsea and they're one of the teams I look out for.

Arsenal

Probably one of the best firms in the 80s. I do rate them. They came to Forest three years on the trot and we had a bit of a thing going with them for a few years. They always done well at Forest and we've always done well down there. They always came looking for it and always had an impressive mob. I put them right up there with your West Hams and Man Utds. In my book, they were in the top 5 in all the country. They were good and had 200 lads who were as game as fuck, with 100 black lads in their firm.

Man United

Always been good with huge numbers. Manchester is an hour and a half away from Nottingham. We had the Kilburn High Street row with them where on the day we got well turned over and murdered. We had the Ferry row with them. We've done well against them over the years. We played against them in the 6th round of the F.A. Cup and 250 of us were at Manchester Piccadilly at 11 o'clock in the morning. Chelsea had a mob at Man City the same day. The season after, we went there 50 handed and drank in all their pubs, but we saw nothing of them all day until we reached the Forecourt outside the ground and a few of them were there gobbing off. That Cup game we took 12,000 fans there and United fans were chanting at us.

"You're One Season Wonders."

One of their top boys said to me that if we turned up the following season, that would show we had bollocks and had bottle. That says it all.

Everton

We've never really had a lot to do with Everton. We had the row that season when they accused us of attacking normal fans in a mini bus at our place. The following season we played them in the first game and we took a bus up there and the Old Bill grabbed me and strip-searched me, all because I was involved in the mini bus case. Everton's a naughty place to go to. I've heard on the grapevine that they've taken good firms down to London, Middlesborough and Newcastle, but they've never really come to Forest in big numbers. But I've got respect for them and on their day they're a force to be reckoned with. I'm now good friends with Andy Nicholls, the author of the Everton book, Scally, which is a worthwhile read.

Liverpool

They've never really come to Forest. A few of our older lads have said that in the late 70s a few of their boys got a bit of a kicking at our place. But the City of Liverpool is a dodgy place to go to. Around '83 about 80 of us walked around outside the ground and 30 of us managed to get into the Anfield Road seats where a lot of their boys sat. We got in there five minutes after kick-off and all the seats were taken. They sussed out we were Forest straight away and tea and coffee cups, and coins, came raining down at us as the whole section stood up. We were up against a wall as they moved towards us. A couple of ours got nicked, a few jumped the wall into the Forest section the other side, some melted into the crowds, and what was left was thrown out by the Scouse Old Bill. After the game about 50 of us went to Southport for a night out. It's on the coast, about 15 miles up the road from Liverpool. Everton had played away at Coventry that day and a few of their lads stopped off in Southport on their way back. The first we heard that they was about was when we were in a nightclub on the end of the pier and a few of them came in and there was a few of them hanging about outside, and there was a bit of a scuffle. Nothing major or anything to write home about.

Bolton

They had a decent firm in the 70s and we took two buses up there one season. Then we never played them for a while until we met them in a League Cup match, in a night game. They turned up 100 handed and gave it the big one on Trent Bridge. I didn't get down there until it was all over but fair play to them, they came. In the 2nd leg up at their place I ran a couple of mini buses and a few lads went up and followed us in their cars. We all met up in 'The Tavern' in the town in Nottingham city centre and we got carried away and got the taste of the beer and never left till about 6.30 p.m. A few of the lads said "fuck it, forget it", but I said, "No, fuck it, we're going," so off we went arriving 20 minutes before the end of the game. We pulled up outside their main boozer, right next to the ground. The rest of the Forest fans were still inside watching the game. A few of their boys came out of the pub as they saw us pull up, next minute there's 30 of them standing in front of us. One of our lot throws something towards them and it hits a lad on the head and knocks him spark out, and we run them back to the pub. More Bolton came out and Forest start coming out of the ground and there's a right battle going on in the car park. We backed them off to the Forecourt and the Old Bill break it up wielding their truncheons. It was complete mayhem before the coppers restored order. We were escorted back to our vans and where we found that some cunt had slashed all the tyres. We were going nowhere, the Old Bill couldn't get us out of town and we were fucked, and we were stranded, not knowing what to do. A white, Opel car kept driving past with some youths in it.

"Come into the town" one shouted out of the window, as it done another circle past us. We let the cunts have it as we bricked the windows. The car skidded as the driver, shocked by the sudden barrage, lost control and headed towards a petrol station where he stopped just short of the petrol pumps. A couple of coppers saw what happened and nicked Pele and Lindo, a couple of our black lads. The Bolton lads came back and pointed them out. Bolton have a good home firm but away, they're not really anything to be honest. I've been back a few times and they've got a good few lads and they rate themselves, but talk to Burnley, Man City, Man Utd, Blackburn, Preston and none of them rate them. I knew a few of their main lads from my time doing the demolition work up there with my uncle. And I next saw a few of them up in Glasgow for the Scotland v England game where a mob of them had just had a row with a mob of West Ham, down near the Barrowlands area of the city. They were shitting themselves and, were in a bit of a panic after 80 of them had just been run, everywhere so their arses were on the floor. I missed it but just caught the tail end of it, but they were dead worried that day and were pleased to see me and the Forest lads.

Middlesbrough

A top class firm who I rate. We've had a few ding-dongs with them and they are one of the best, home or away. They can do it, they've got some decent lads. They are the business, in my top 6. They are an organised firm. Forest had lots of trouble with them in the late 70s and into the 80s, but they always turn up at Forest. We had the Battle of Thornaby up there in 95/96. I've got nothing but respect for them.

Spurs

Very underestimated, I always thought it was a rough place to go to. We took a mob down there on the service train, around 95/96 and drank in a pub near the ground. There was about 60 of us and a few Tottenham lads kept walking past and clocking us, but it was early and they wanted to have a go but they couldn't get a mob together. After the game they had a huge mob waiting on the Seven Sisters Road. They started mingling in with us and gobbing off. One particular little midget was giving me a hard time with his mouth.

"Hang on," I told him, "we've been here since 11 o'clock this morning," and I told the cunt to piss off. We passed a pub with people drinking outside and they saw us and peppered us with bottles and glasses. The Old Bill let the dogs go and more Spurs fans mixed in with us. If it weren't for the Old Bill we might well have come unstuck. They've come a few times up to us and there's been a few little things, but they failed to show up in the F.A. Cup replay last season.

They played Leeds away a few years back and on their way back to London they stopped off in a pub in Nottingham, and they came well unstuck. They were 40 handed and got chased all around town. We then played them the next season in a Cup game and they were frothing at the mouth, out for revenge, but the game was snowed off and they smashed a pub up, With no one in, we waited in town at the pub they'd got battered at, and we had huge numbers out that day. They put all the windows in at the pub they attacked, and C.S. gassed a couple of old codgers sitting there drinking their halves of bitter.

Aston Villa

Very overrated, a gang of bullies and what's all that shit with them and them Mackem cunts? They've come to Forest twice and got hammered one year, proper slaughtered. I don't rate them at all.

Man City

Never really had a lot to do with them myself, but the older lads say that when we won the League in the late 70s, they had a tough time up there. They said it was right rough up there. They always bring loads of fans up to Forest but they've never come in a big mob and come looking for it. We've never had a right toe-to-toe with them. I can remember their mob, The Cool Cats, and they probably think that we're not worth turning out for.

Charlton

They came to Forest in a night game in the early 80s and had a mob of 30 big lads in leather jackets, and by all accounts they give it the biggen down by the cricket ground. I've been down there twice with Forest and never seen anything, but they must have some boys because in that night game they more than held their own on Radcliff Road.

Blackburn

Have they got a firm? I've met a few of them at England games and they reckon they've got 40 to 50 lads. I've been up there a few times with Forest and I've never seen them. We took 150 up there and took over the town. There was a rumour that they once bought a mob to us in a F.A. Cup game and were out on London Road looking for a row.

Birmingham

Another team I rate from personal experience and in my opinion they're the best in the Midlands. They remind me a bit of Boro. They're game, well organised, and well up for it. We've had our run ins with them over the years and they're always there when you want it.

Newcastle

I've a lot, of good friends up there. I went to Feynoord in a European game with them and they had a 300 strong mob out that day. It was like going to an England game. I've been at least half a dozen times with them to Sunderland, home and away, and I've never seen Sunderland do well against them. A few of us Forest lads met up in Amsterdam with the Geordies and two trainloads of us went into Rotterdam Central. We came off and the police baton-charged us back into the station and back to the stop where the stadium was. The mob was a mixture of young and old and on that day I'd put them up against anyone, the train load before us managed to slip past the Old Bill at the Central station and had it with a firm of Feynoord. A Newcastle copper who was out there on spotting duty stopped me and asked what I was doing out there.

"What you doing Gary? You're on an international banning order."

I said, "No I'm not, I'm banned from Forest and England."

They scratched their heads and didn't have an answer and in the end they made me take my baseball cap off and took some photos of me. I didn't have a ticket to get in so they didn't have a clue what to do with me. They were on their radios and then they stood around scratching their heads while they waiting for a reply. They didn't know whether to nick me or not, or let me go. They didn't know what exactly the law was. About 15 of us without match tickets were put on a train back to Amsterdam. I just acted dumb and it worked. I've seen the Geordie lads first hand and it's been an evil place to go to. The Forest lads said in the 70s we played them in a 6th round F.A. Cup game and it was abandoned because of a pitch invasion which was supposedly led by a 56 year old, eighteen stone, bald Geordie. The game was replayed at Goodison Park two weeks later and finished 0-0. 3 days later at the replay at the same venue we went out by the odd goal, losing 1-0. The Geordies are good people and I won't have a bad word said about them. In days gone by no one, really went up there. The Geordies always seem to be Man Mountains in their donkey jackets and heavy work boots.

Portsmouth

In the mid 80s they had a really good firm and came to Forest two or three times. They turned up in a League Cup game 200 handed and that was good because it was a night game. They came in our seats and it went mental. We had a blinding row with them and not many teams have done that. We used to sit in the section next to the away fans but Pompey came bowling in our bit and was well up for it. We didn't expect them to come into our seats, we were all in there and they came in with all the latest gear on and the shout went up "they're here," and it went up in the air. Afterwards on Trent Bridge it was toe-to-toe. It was wave after wave of attacks on one another. It was a proper row.

A couple of seasons back we took two busloads and a few cars down there and we stopped in Fareham, about 10 miles from Pompey. We phoned them and called it on but all they said was "come into Portsmouth." I was on a banning order and spoke to them on the phone but they was insistent that we came to Fratton. In the end I got pissed off with this cunt on the other end of the line making excuses.

"Stay there, we're coming," I ranted down the phone.

Half an hour later we was getting off the train and out on to the street, and it went off all the way down the road from the station to the ground. No one had a ticket to get in the ground and the coppers got sick of our lot hanging around, outside, and causing trouble and not going in the match, so they rounded us up and we were back in our buses and away by 3.30 in the afternoon. Years ago we played them the first game of the season and they turned up 60 handed and drank in The Queens Hotel, which faces the railway station. There was trouble outside the ground with them and there was the odd scuffle, but I think by then they were pass their sell by date. But saying that my mates in Newcastle said that Pompey turned up two years on the trot 30 handed, at 11 o'clock in the morning and got off the service train and had a row outside the pub facing the station. My mate reckons it was the same 30 lads two years on the bounce. They were as game as anything so you've got to rate them.

Fulham

Have they got any boys? I went there in the 70s when I was a kid, in the F.A. Cup. We didn't play them for years and a couple of years ago we played them on a Bank holiday so 40 of us went down on the train. We drank around Putney Bridge and then went in the game, for 10 minutes and then we were bored shitless so we fucked off, and we never see a lad all day. They've never been up to our place. I think they're worse than Watford and Blackburn by the sounds of it.

Crystal Palace

We've had a few rows with them and they came to Forest in a Simod Cup semi final. They bought about four thousand fans up for that game. They came up the road about 30 handed and we bumped straight into them. There wasn't that many of us out that night, but we had a good 2-minute toe-to-toe with them. In the 80s we played them in the F.A. Cup down there and it was the middle of winter and there was snow everywhere. As soon as we got out of the couple of mini buses we ran down there, they were on us and attacked us, so they have got a few lads.

Norwich

We've been there a few times and we just swamp them with our numbers, but they turn out. They played up north at somewhere like Everton, and they stopped off in Nottingham on their way back and drank in The Flying Horse, which at the time was one of our main pubs. There was about 50 of them and we heard they were in there and Forest attacked the pub. I remember they had a big skinhead with them and he had a spiders web tattooed on his head, but they gave as good as they got and came out all guns firing, lobbing glasses and bottles.

West Brom

I don't rate them. They're a bit like Aston Villa. We've been in their end and took the piss. They came to us in the mid 80s and had 70 lads on Trent Bridge but we had a European game the following week so our lads didn't bother turning out. So they've been once in the 25 years I've been going. They turned up in Newcastle for their last game of the season about 50 handed, and gave it the biggen but normally they don't travel too well, a lot of them teams from the Midlands have a high opinion of themselves but most are tin-pot firms.

Southampton

We've had a couple of things with them and 20 to 30 of them come to us once in a Cup game. All they done was gobbed off in the seats next to us. They're all red and white striped shirts and loads of mouth. They went to Notts County on the last day of the season and came up in two mini buses. I was out with my girlfriend in town that night and they were drinking in the square.

I took a bus down there in '95 and we were in Southampton at 11 o'clock in the morning. My mate John from Sheffield organised the hire of the bus and told the owners we were going on a shopping trip to France. We never went in the match but drank in the pubs around the old Dell. After the game a few of their lads tried to come into the pub we were drinking in, and they got chased out. Some even tried to hide in the toilet, what I've seen of them I don't rate them. I hear they don't even turn out when they play their near neighbours, Portsmouth, and that stupid fucking "When the Saints go Marching In" song they sing. That's enough to do your brain in. I bumped into a mob of theirs on England duty out in Berlin. I was on my way out to Poland in '91 and they had a firm in The Sports Bar. Most of them had ski hats and bubble coats on. They looked the part; I'll give them that. They looked like Man Utd or someone.

Sunderland

I've got my hat-trick of nickings up there and they've got a lot of lads at home and I've come unstuck there a couple of times. But Forest have been up there and done the business, we've always had rows with them and always had this thing with them, even before I met the Newcastle lads. They once came to Forest 50 handed and attacked The Fountain pub. 20 of us chased them everywhere. We then played them another time on the last day of the season, and their firm, The Seaburn Casuals, came down. They had a lad with them dressed in a poncho. He thought he was Clint Eastwood, the prick. He even had a Mexican hat on. They got hammered outside the cricket ground after the game, seventy of them gave it the biggen and the Old Bill saved them. It was a massacre and they got well fucked. 300 or 400 of us were out waiting for them. The week before it had been all over our local papers that The Seaburn Casuals were coming for trouble and that bit of free advertising saved me phoning everyone to get them out. We were well up for it. Our friendship with Newcastle now has taken it up another level.

Wigan

They've got a tight little mob and I know a few of them. I was drinking with some of them up in Scotland for the England play off games. We once took 150 lads to Wigan because I think it was the first time we'd ever played them. Mansfield went there a few years back on the last day of the season, and Wigan had 300 lads out waiting for them. I've heard on the grapevine that they're game. They came to Forest with 70 lads and looked for a row outside the ground. We'd all just got our banning orders so we couldn't get near them at the ground.

Ipswich

Two bob, as Bill Gardner would say. They came with 30 lads to Forest in a Cup game once, and in the 70s our lads had it with them in a Cup replay at their place, and the boys said they had a few black lads that were game. They had a couple of black brothers that ran the show down there for a few years. When we got relegated and we went there the last game of the season, they had a mob of mainly black and half-caste lads and one of them's meant to be the brother of an ex Ipswich and Tottenham player. Guess who? We took over the whole town that day and invaded the pitch at the end.

Preston

We went to Blackpool the night before we played them and took 150 boys over there. 30 of us never went in and we drank all around the town before, during and after the game, and they're meant to have a few lads with a bit of a reputation but that day we never see anyone. We walked around like we owned the place, plus they've never been to Forest.

Derby

They've got 50 good lads but they're all dreamers. No matter what we've done, they've always done better. They're the best on the planet, they've never been done and never been run. They're the hardest set of lads in the world. They think they are just fantastic. Whatever happened or whatever you say, they are better than you, full stop. They are better than anyone else, that's all you get from them. So there's no point in talking about them.

West Ham

They were the bees' knees, the bollocks in the 80s. No one could touch them. There's only one team ever that's come to Forest and totally taken the piss, and that was West Ham. They once came into our seats and run Forest onto the pitch. I had to sign on at the police station at 3 o'clock and I used to get down to the ground normally for the last half an hour or twenty minutes. When I got there this day, the lads were still in shock. Three years on the spin they came into Broadmarsh bus station and cleared it. They'd come straight off the train and do the business. It was embarrassing. They were a proper organised firm; they were the dog's bollocks.

Sheffield United

Sheffield's a rough, difficult place to go to. It's only an hour up the road from Nottingham so we've always travelled there, and they've got some good lads. In the 70s our older lads gave them a run for their money in the Shoreham End. Forest used to have some right ding-dongs with them. Stephen Julian Cedric Cowans writes in his book about how 80 of them came to Forest and gave it to us but they had darts, pool balls and all sorts of weapons. What he fails to remember and write about is the times we've gone there and done the business. A convenient memory that? I know a lot of their lads through me mate John.

Millwall

Millwall, they never disappoint. They came to Forest in the early 90s in a League Cup game and was sitting in a pub in the city centre, 60 handed. We tried to attack the pub and the coppers turned up and stopped it when they tried to shift the mob from the pub, the Millwall lads inside barricaded themselves in and smashed the windows as they hurled gear at the coppers from inside. There was a bit of a siege going on there. When the Old Bill did get in they searched the pub and found axes, knives and Stanley blades, all hidden in the toilets and down the back of the seats.

The season after the documentary they came to us big time, 300 strong on a service train. We had two big mobs out that day, 150 met over in Netherfield on the outskirts of Nottingham. We knew what time Millwall's train arrived from London so we timed it so that we caught a local train that arrived in Nottingham at bang on the same time. All went well until a police helicopter sussed us, so the Millwall train was held up outside the station. The train we were on was allowed to come into the station and waiting for us was the coppers. As we tried to leave the station, they baton-charged us but the lads were having none of it and steamed into the Old Bill, chasing them out of the station. The other mob of ours was in the town centre. It don't bear thinking about but if the Old Bill hadn't have rumbled our plans it would have been a row made in heaven. A T.V. crew went around all day filming with the police and they showed their shots from the helicopter and the rest of the day's events on a, ten-minute news special on Central T.V. But as for them coming in their thousands, that's never happened. But for the square mile they must have more nutters than any other team. They're crackers. A couple of our lads over the years have become friends with a couple of their top boys. I think we'd hold our own against them and I think they rate Forest.

Stoke City

We had a bit of a thing with them in the early 80s and they cut a couple of our lads. Then we didn't play them for years and then I'd just got married, around '95, and the F.A. Cup draw was live on Match of the Day, and they pulled out Forest and Stoke. I went fucking mad and was jumping up and down like a nutter. My missus just sat there shaking her head and looking at me like I'd totally lost the plot.

"What's the matter with ya? Sit down."

"You don't understand, we've just drawn Stoke City in the Cup," I said.

"Whatever."

It was like a scene from The Football Factory when Frank Harper's character is watching Osgood and Hudson do the F.A. Cup draw and out comes Chelsea v Millwall. I couldn't sleep that night, as I was so excited.

A buzz went around Nottingham weeks before the game and on the day we took a massive mob over there. It's only an hour from us so it was a bit of a Derby game. Most of us went over by car and we plotted up in a pub. It's like going back in time with all the Victorian houses and factory chimneys. It's another tough area, which breeds tough men. Nearly everyone had a sheepskin coat or donkey jacket on. The Old Bill didn't have a clue. A few of their lads came to the pub we were in and I clumped this youth outside, and he went backwards into some road works and fell down an open manhole. They're fucking nuts, though. At the end of the game, we all came out with 5 minutes to go and a mob of Stoke's, youngsters steamed into us. We had four thousand fans in the top tier in the stand behind the goal. We ran them off to the right and ran them back into their section of the ground. We went back out onto the street and we were right up for it as the adrenalin was pumping. I looked around and felt good. We had a good mob here. It was pitch black and a mob of them appeared in front of us. A roar went up and we ran them everywhere. From behind us came a mob of their older lads so we turned to face them. A big cunt in a sheepskin stepped towards me and I threw a punch but missed him, but the force and power of it pulled my arm out of its socket. I was on the floor in agony and have never felt pain like it. I had tears in my eyes I can tell you. The Old Bill got round me and couldn't work out what had happened. A few of our lads had stopped with me and the coppers were asking what had gone on. They just shrugged their shoulders and didn't answer. Some Stoke lads walking past didn't know what had gone on and were gobbing off.

"That'll teach you to come to Stoke."

They thought I'd been put on my arse with a punch. An ambulance arrived and I was helped into the back of it. Another one of our lads was already in the back as he'd been knocked down and trodden on by a police horse.

In the hospital was one of our old lads, who had been stabbed in the arm with a screwdriver. My arm was pushed back into its socket but I didn't feel a thing, as I was as high as a kite on drugs. Not mine, the ones the hospital gave to me.

The next day me and me mate, Daryl, who stayed with me, caught a taxi back to Nottingham and we went straight down The Friar Tuck pub where my missus was working behind the bar, she took one look at me all strapped up and shook her head and walked off to serve somebody else. Throwing that right-hander cost me dearly. I had no money coming in for nearly 3 months and I suppose it cost me my marriage because after that things were never the same between her and me. She used to sometimes moan about me going to football but I think this was one of the many straws that broke the camel's back. If I'd have caught the bloke with that punch I'd thrown, I swear he would have landed on the other side of the moon. The boys said they had some right battles in and around that grave-yard on the walk back to the station, and in the replay at our place they came looking for it, but our lot was over at The Meadows Estate fighting with the Old Bill. In the disturbance, a copper got a slab put over his head and ended up in hospital. Stoke have got a major mob who are as game as fuck and two of their main lads, the Mills brothers, come from Nottingham so things have calmed down a bit lately. Now there's mutual respect and there's no longer any hatred between the firms, although we do have one important thing in common. They hate Derby County as much as we do.

Wolves

We had a few rows with them years ago, as everybody did. I remember as a kid in 1980 we played them in the League Cup final at Wembley and I remember seeing The Forest Mad Squad, as our mob was then known, having a bit of a row with a Wolves firm on Wembley Way. I was with me dad and I remember most of our lads had on the green, nylon flight jackets with the orange coloured lining inside. We went there in '83 with a small mob of Forest and we went in their seats. It was going off all through the first half and down at the tea bar at half time. After the game the Wolves firm got their act together and ran us up the road. The rest of our lads came out of the Forest section and we had a bit of a row with them. I was 15 and a right gobby little shit so they wanted to kill me.

They've got a decent home firm who are no mugs but they're not the best I've seen, plus they always seem to be covered in Burberry or Aquascutum check gear. You find 70 year old geezers at Wolves wearing snide Burberry shirts and baseball caps. Most of the fake Burberry gear from Thailand must end up in Wolverhampton. They love all that shit up there. They once came 130 handed to Forest and it nearly went off on the bridge, and another time we were playing them at our place and they came off the motorway on a bus and headed towards where we were drinking in Clifton. They then stopped in a pub, which was just a five minute walk from the pub we were in, and then for some unknown reason our coppers turned up and sussed out what was going on. We were on the phone to one another and didn't realise just how close we were to one another. The distance between the two clubs is only an hour's drive apart but for some reason we've never really met head on.

Leeds

We've always done well up there. Once, after a game, 80 of us attacked their main pub, 'Jackabellas', which is in the Bond Street shopping area. We got away from the Old Bill in dribs and drabs and when we got to the city centre we all came together. About 40 of them saw us coming and came out of the pub at us. We hit them with everything as road, work cones caved in all the windows, and we ran them everywhere. We've always done all right up there. I've been up there 40 handed and we've performed well. They've come a couple of times to Forest and one year they came in a massive mob and we got locked in the pub as they gave it the biggen on Trent Bridge. We couldn't get out so we had it in the doorway of the pub with the Old Bill. In the 70s, they were good and were like Man Utd with the numbers, and then in the 80s you had The Service Crew, which was active. Ye Leeds have always had some decent lads.

Q.P.R.

A lot of people might laugh at this, but in the early 80s we had some right rows with them three or four years on the trot down there, and on more than one occasion on the park they more than held their own. We once went there 200 strong on the service train using the Persil tickets, that was around '84, time. We went into their end, and came out at half time and stood back down with the rest of the Forest, in the away. After the game we came out and turned left past the flats, and as we came out onto the main road there, they were 200 of them walking towards us. It went off, bang right in the middle of the road with both teams not backing off as it went solid toe-to-toe. Coppers on horseback had to ride in between us to split up the fighting.

The following year we came unstuck a bit as 40 of us got chased across the park, but Rangers had a good firm out that day with plenty of numbers. I ran so far and then stopped and looked around. Behind me was some idiot that had been chasing me and he was in striking distance so I gave him a punch, and he went flying through the air. We then held them off by the gate with our black lad, Pele, at the front with me.

"Get the nigger, get the Spade," they were shouting.

Pele punched one straight on the nose and he went backwards, losing his footing and landed in the pile of police horse shit, everyone just burst out laughing as this prick laid in a pile of steaming hot horse turds. The Old Bill rounded us up and put us on the tube and waiting on the opposite platform was Gregor and his cronies. As the train pulled in, they came over and tried to get on and mingle in with us. A couple of them flashed blades and gobbed off, but the Old Bill sussed them and fucked them off out of it. Every time we played them and there was trouble, that little Gregor, was always in the thick of it. But they've only ever come to Forest once and that was in a League Cup quarter-final, and we won 5-2. They bought a busload but all they did was come on the bridge after the match and fired a flare into our lot, which hit me. The Old Bill rounded them up and fucked them off back on the bus, and they've not been seen in Nottingham since. We enjoyed going down there because we were guaranteed a row, but they've never ever done anything away from home. To be rated you have to be able to do both home and away. Ask any Forest lads and they'll tell you the same about Rangers.

Burnley

Basically I can't stand them. I've had one or two things going on with them but since that youth from Forest got killed up there the other year, my dislike for them has got worse. I was on a 3-year banning order when that happened and I wasn't allowed in the game so I had a few drinks in a pub and then decided to walk up towards the ground. I nipped into some flats and had a piss around the back, out of the way, and as I finished I noticed a dozen or so lads had clocked me. I knew they were Burnley lads and I was on my own but there was no way I was going to run off, so I casually walked back to where my car was. They came up behind me and next minute one of them whacked me with a punch on the back of my head. I had my back to them so to me that says it all, the fucking bullies. I stopped and they stopped.

"Come on," I said to the crowd of them, "let's have it one on to one if you're so brave."

I couldn't understand what they said because they speak a mixture of English and Martian. They mumbled something but weren't so brave when I stood my ground.

They came to Forest 30 handed in the League Cup in the 80s, and they gave it the biggen, but the coppers got hold of them.

"Come to Burnley in the 2nd leg," said one of their many big mouths and we did and went up there 80 handed, arriving at 5 o'clock, and drank in the two pubs facing the train station. We got a nod from them at 7 o'clock telling us to go to the 'Yates' Bar. We walked straight through the doors and give it to them and they went everywhere. Quite a few of them leapt the bar to get away and the 40 of them that were in there completely bottled it. The Old Bill arrived and we got outside and split into smaller mobs, and as we walked towards the ground, groups of Burnley stood on street corners, mouthing off. As soon as we walked up to them, they backed off. A group of youths stood in the middle of the road, chanting, "Su Su Suicide Squad, Su Su Suicide Squad," as I walked up to them, I said, "Don't worry about all that old bollocks, we're Forest and we're here," They fucking shit themselves and didn't know what to say. They're all fucking arseholes. We'd hit their pub and they had no answer.

A few weeks after the 17-year-old Forest lad got killed up there, we played Preston. I had me mum and dad over my place one night and was upstairs doing something and I went down to answer a knock on the front door. Standing there were two coppers, one from Nottingham and the other from Burnley. They hand me a letter, which said that if I were caught in Burnley after the Preston game then I would be arrested, blah, blah, blah. They went around to most of our lads and handed these letters out. They thought we would be out for revenge after this Preston game, which is only about half an hour away from Burnley. But to me, Burnley are just another over rated tin-pot mob.

Plymouth

They have some good lads and they once came 50 handed to Forest in about 95/96. They were swanning around the bridge before the game and looked the part, though some of their lads were quiet young, some maybe 10 years younger than me. Afterwards they came right unstuck outside the cricket ground. About 30 of us older lot give it to them and a few of them were sprawled out as the rest of the others backed off whilst telling one another to stand. I've never been down there myself but the lads who went down in a couple of mini-buses said they turned out big time for us. In the car park after the game, the lads said it came on top a bit and if it wasn't for the Old Bill they could have come unstuck. One of our young lads now lives down in the West Country and has got to know a few of their lads. He's bought a couple of them up to a few Forest games and they seem decent lads. I've been there on a night out but I've never been there for the football. But you have to give their firm some credit because for most away games they have to travel a fair old distance. I wouldn't underestimate them. Most teams that go down there looking for it get it. They've got a big catchment area for their support so they're bound to have some good lads who are up for it.

Leicester City

We've had some right rows with them over the years but we've always had the upper hand. They look the part and dress the part, they always have done. I know a few of their lads and they're decent, the likes of Dolby, Ashley, Bert, Drew, and both the Jonnos. They've some good lads who over the years I've met in prison and at England games. They've had a reputation over the years but the thing what done me was when they joined up with Derby and called themselves The Derby-Leicester Alliance (D.L.A.) so that they could take us on. How can you take a firm seriously that joins up with your archrivals?

Cardiff

We've only really started playing them over the last couple of seasons but the last time we played them they bought a mob to Forest and when we played them in the return fixture in Cardiff, we took a hell of a firm down there, but because of the coppers nothing really happened. I'm now good friend with a couple of their boys, Deacon and H. We first met out in Thailand. Deacon's been up here for a drink a few times and I've been down there, but you have to give it to them, they're a good firm with huge numbers. They've done it all around the country so they deserve the respect. It's a big city with one team with a massive support so they're right up there with the best of them. One of their main lads came up from Cardiff in his flash car when they played us, and some of the lads followed him into Nottingham after they spotted him in Clifton, on the outskirts of the city. He parked up near to The Ocean nightclub with a few lads in a convoy of Cardiff cars. Waiting just across the road in one of the canal side pubs was a mob of Forest, 70 handed, and it went mental as these 30 Cardiff went at it toe-to-toe, and by all accounts gave as good as they got. After the Old Bill turned up and the Cardiff lot were escorted away, some of ours went back to the Cardiff cars and proceeded to smash the windows and slash the tyres. Apparently Mr A was not best pleased when he returned after the game to find his flash motor trashed. It was taken away later that night on the back of a tow truck.

Watford

Not worth talking about. I got nicked there, once for running on the pitch. Them two dickhead brothers, the Brimsons, follow Watford and if they do have any boys they must cringe when they hear them two cunts spouting off. Having your head shaved and wearing a Stone Island jumper five years after they've gone out of fashion does not qualify you to be a football hooligan. They're fucking embarrassing, total nobheads.

Coventry

Another team that in the 80s we've had some good rows with. They've got a few lads and they've been to Forest once and were in our town centre at 6 o'clock at night. They turned up in cars and had a bit of a scuffle with a few of our lads and one of ours was slashed across the hand with a knife. A few times, we've been down there and totally took the piss, and then again, we've been down there and they've turned out for us. But they've never been to Forest in any sort of numbers. I did hear that they turned up in Newcastle recently for an F.A. Cup game and were looking for a row. Perhaps they've joined up with Derby and Leicester and are now known as the C.D.L. Alliance.

Brighton

I recently got turned over there but these are crafty bastards. They don't turn out during the day but at night they're like rats and come out when they know that the bulk of the visiting fans have fucked off home. We took the piss there all day and were in one of their pubs up near the railway station, when in walked a lad who turned out to be a Jock. He was handing out some leaflets about a book or something that he had coming out. He told us where to go later on if we fancied a row with a mob of locals. He told us that because of the Old Bill the Brighton lads hadn't been able to get near us. I was in the toilet when he first came in and one of our lads shouted to me that a geezer wanted to speak to me. He told me he was a Hibs fan that lived down there and he knew all the Brighton lads. He told me where to meet them later and we'd get it on. I said "O.K., no problem, we'll definitely be there." As the night carried on our numbers dwindled down from 30 to just 12 of us that were staying in Brighton for the night. He gave one of the lads his number, and at about 8 o'clock, we rang him and he told us where to go. When we got to the pub, where we were to meet there was no one in there, no sign at all of them. We were all dressed up in our nightclub gear and best shiney shoes and really thought, this was all bollocks and that we'd been sent on a wild goose chase. A few of the lads got chatting to a few local birds and were engrossed in them, a couple were powdering their noses in the gents and a couple sat watching the pub telly. I looked out the window and noticed about 30 lads coming towards us from a pub opposite. Four or five of us came out the main doors and walked towards them and straight away they didn't want to know as they backed off. I chinned a couple and done the Scotsman, but then they realised how many of us there actually was. I could see them stop and I could see their brains ticking over. They then changed direction and came at us. As I walked backwards in my leather- soled shoes, I slipped and went arse over tit on the kerb. That was it, they were all over me and I couldn't get to my feet. I was fucked. I couldn't move as their boots landed on my head and around my ribs. I thought I was about to die, I thought "this is it." I hadn't been on the floor for years but fair play to a Brighton lad. He'd seen enough and stepped in and called a halt to it God knows what would have happened if he hadn't of. The rest of the lads I was with ran back into the pub and the windows got smashed as Brighton attacked the pub. Fred, one of our young lot, held the door with a fire extinguisher and cracked a few with that. I was left, dazed, standing on the pavement behind this Brighton mob. I did think about going back into them from behind but thought I'd better leave it and just get out of the way, which I did. I saw one of their half-caste lads waving a blade about, and one of ours had his arm broken. As soon as the coppers' sirens could be heard, these Brighton lads were off and back down their boltholes. They've never ever been to Forest, but I think they'd get it big time if they dared to turn up.

Rotherham

Not worth talking about, we went there the last game of the season, and we were all on banning orders and we never saw one of their lads all day long, another invisible firm. I recently went with Cass up to Rotherham to do a book signing and three lads turned up so I don't know how they have this reputation. They've never turned up at our place so I suppose it's all part of the Rotherham myth.

Luton

Been there a couple of times and we had it with them the first game of the season. We took two mini-buses and had it with them in the town centre after the game, there were battles in the middle of the road as we jumped out and had it with them. We played them in the League Cup final at Wembley in '89 and we were scrapping with them outside the turnstiles. One of them threw a scalding hot cup of coffee in my face, which burnt like fuck, and I wasn't very happy. 150 of us had been down the night before but the first time we spotted them was on the day in Wembley Way. For the numbers they've got they're quiet game. They've been to Notts County a few times, supposedly looking for us, but what I can't understand is why go to Notts County and not come to us when they're playing us. Enough said. A few years back they took 80 lads to Mansfield and 30 Forest lads went over. They attacked Mansfield's main pub at 11 o'clock in the morning but we never got there till late so by the time we got there the Old Bill were wrapped around them. After the game, we saw them back at the railway station and they saw us and threw stones at us over the fence, but I can't knock them, they turned up.

Hull City

This is one team in my career that I've always wanted to play and we haven't played them since the 70s. They're a hooligan's dream side, but we've never crossed swords with them. We get a few Hull lads come down to watch Forest and they seem nice lads. Mansfield turned up there 30 handed and Hull turned out 150 lads for them so you've got to respect them. They surrounded Mansfield and threw bricks and everything they could lay their hands on, and the Old Bill just seemed to let them get on with it. We drove pass their pub, The Silver Cod, on the way to the ground and hundreds of them poured out to follow us up the road. They're as game as fuck. If we'd had played Hull 5 years before we got our banning orders it would have been interesting.

Tranmere

They've come to Forest with a mob on a Monday night I think it was, and it was called off. A few of our lads were drinking in Yates wine bar and this Tranmere mob attacked them. There were 10 of our lot and about 30 of them. I've been up there a couple of times and we've been in their seats, but we've never seen their boys, but apparently they have got some.

Sheffield Wednesday

Not that keen on them. I suppose it's because of my Blades connections. I'll give it to them, they've been to Forest two years on the bounce and they were in 'The Flying Horse' and we attacked them, and they held us off by throwing bottles and glasses. The year after I was up in Sheffield with me mate, John, for a weekend, and on the same day Wednesday were playing at Forest. They turned up in a mob and got chased by our boys from 'The Dog and Bear' pub to the market', which is about half a mile. One of them got his leg broken but by all accounts, they got well battered. I've been to Wednesday that many times and you always have to go looking for them. A Wednesday lad has just bought a book out and he makes out that the couple of times they've been down our place and that they've turned us over. Dream on son.

Bristol City

We had a right row with them in the semis of the League Cup in '89. They came to Forest 200 strong. I'd just come back from Turkey and out there me and me mate John got chatting to a lad on a bus who said he was a Bristol City fan. John told him he was from Sheffield and the bloke nodded his head and said, "you've got a good firm." John pointed at me. "Gary's from Nottingham," he said. "You ain't got much of a mob have you?" he said. I thought "you cunt" but I kept my mouth shut and didn't really say a lot.

On the day we played them I'd seen them come past the cricket ground and so I mingled in with them.
"They've got no boys" I heard a couple of them say in that stupid farmers' accent they've got, we came to the bookmakers on the corner on the way to the ground and I could see a few familiar Forest faces hanging about. As we turned the corner, there they were, all our boys were spread out in the road and it was our top firm. This Bristol mob shit themselves and they were soon on their toes, they got legged everywhere.

When we played them down there we took 200 plus and it pissed down with rain all day. We drank all around the city centre and we never saw them. We headed off towards the ground and as we came to a park, loads of them were sitting on a wall, waiting for us. We came across the park through the trees and we ran them everywhere. They were shit and after the game, they tried to attack us as we came out near the turnstiles. We steamed into them and true to form, they were off. I spotted the cunt from Turkey with them but as I went to grab him and bang him someone else tried to whack him and he took off.
"Who aint got a firm now, you stupid bastard?" I shouted after him, and we chased them everywhere. I've never seen him since but that's no surprise. Don't gob off if you can't back it up.

Doncaster

They have a few lads and Forest have a few lads from up there. One of our old lads from up there, his son is one of Doncaster's boys. The dad is a big lump and has bought a few of their lads down here for a drink on a couple of occasions A few of the Donny lads follow Leeds and they've got a good little firm. I've been up there in a League Cup game but nothing happened. When they were in the Conference League they took mobs everywhere and I used to hear about all their exploits through my Forest and Donny connections.

Huddersfield

I got nicked there in '89 and they've got a game firm and have a good England following. I know Del, one of their main lads, from the England scene. I also know John, one of theirs, whose now got a bar out in Thailand. I always have a drink with him when I'm out in Pattaya. They've turned up at Mansfield a couple of times and they're no mugs. We've got them the first game of the season so that should be fun.

Bradford

We played them not long after a fire tragically destroyed their ground so the game with us was played at the nearby Oddsaul rugby stadium, and fucking hell, what a night that was. It was chaos and one of the best nights I've ever had at football. It went off big time. We all arranged to meet at the nearest pub to the train station and when a few of us got there it was full of their boys. This was around 5 o'clock, and a couple of hours before the evening kick-off. We didn't really get it together until about half an hour before the match started, and as we walked to the ground in one big firm they came at us from every angle. No wonder their mob's called The Ointment as they were all over us. I was surprised that most of their lads are white, but I'll give it to them, they are game. Afterwards the coppers got on our case and we couldn't really get away so nothing really happened. The following morning the fighting up there made the headlines in the 'Today' newspaper.

Walsall

We played them in the League Cup a few years ago. I never went but the lads I know that did go said they had a 10-minute battle with some of their lads and they reckon it was one of the best rows they've had for years. It came about when our lot arrived in cars and were parking up in some side street and as they walked down towards the ground they just bumped into one another. There was about 30 Forest and 20 Walsall lads but it went off toe-to-toe for a good 10 minutes of pure fighting.

Barnsley

We played them in the season that either they went up to the Premiership or we came down. I can't remember which but we took six thousand fans there and we had it all day long there with them. We tried to get in their end and we nearly did, but then the coppers sussed it. We were still fighting in the town centre an hour after the game had finished. They have some game lads and Barnsley is one of them tough Yorkshire towns where you know you're going to get a row if you fancy one. They came to Forest 40 handed for a Friday night game but they didn't go looking for it. They just give it a bit of a show that's all.

Chesterfield

Not worth talking about. They're another gang of arsehole bullies who are two bob. Mansfield are their archrivals and turn them over every time they meet. Their top boy is a dickhead that calls himself Bungle. The name of him and their so-called firm says it all. Zebedee off the Magic Roundabout would be a better name for him.

Port Vale

Been there a couple of times but never seen anyone. Apparently they're meant to have a mob and they have it with Stoke when they play one another. Another myth mob.

Oldham

They've been to Forest in the early 90s, 60 handed, all with the Stone Island gear on. They didn't go in the game but stayed in a pub near to Notts County's ground. They was all lads around the 30 age group but looked the part. They've also got a big England following and they had a decent mob out in Berlin on their way out to Poland. I know Spence, one of their main lads, again through my Thai connections. I rate Oldham highly. We played them in the League Cup final in 1990 and that's the only Forest Cup final I've ever missed since I've been following them. I was out in New York on holiday, but we had 250 lads out that day and the lads bumped into Oldham's firm outside Wembley Park tube station. I then heard that Oldham knew they were messing with one of the big boys but I do rate Oldham and for a small club they've got some game boys.

Peterborough

Should stick to farming, as they're a gang of fucking idiots. They turn up when they play Notts County and they think they're Jack the Biscuit. We played them the last game of the season a few years back and we took ten thousand fans down there. We were in their town centre all day but where were they that day? They have, got a black lad that follows Leeds that works the pubs and club doors in Peterborough. If I was him I'd stick to following Leeds and let the rest of them stick to their farming. Cambridge, their rivals, have more boys and are a lot better than them.

Wrexham

They've got a few boys. We went up there in a League Cup game and they turned out for us with a decent mob. We couldn't seem to get our act together that night. I walked through the town centre with a few mates and Wrexham were all over the shop looking for us. It looked a bit dodgy at times and to be truthful if it wasn't for the Old Bill we might well have come unstuck, plus if we'd have got ourselves together we could have had a good row.

Stockport

They bought 50 lads in a League Cup match. We always used to look forward to the first and second rounds because we would play teams from the lower divisions who we would never normally play. You knew these smaller teams had lads who would turn up, so you knew there'd be a row. All the games except the final were a night game. Stockport came but they came unstuck on Trent Bridge. I've been up there twice and nothings happened.

Southend

I know a few of their lads from England games. Damien's one of their lads and he's a decent bloke. A few years back we went there for the first game of the season. We got down there the night before, 200 handed, and we didn't see a single one of their lads, we took the place over, we ran amock. I don't know anything about their actual firm because I've never seen them in action. One good thing to come out of Southend is Stan Collymore. Forest signed him and to me he's one of the best players ever to put on a Forest shirt. He was a great signing. We didn't pay a lot for him but to me he's the best centre forward we've ever had.

Swansea

I've never been down there but they came up to us in the early 80s. A couple of vanloads of Swansea were drinking in 'The Crown' pub, near the station. Our lot have gone down there and it's kicked off. Two of our lads got nicked and were sent down for it. I've heard on the grapevine that Swansea have a decent firm. We play them this season and most of us lot are on that 10 mile radius ban and that's a pity because it would have been interesting. It would have been one of the highlights of the 05/06 season.

Lincoln

It's only 40 miles from Nottingham and a few of us used to go out for nights out there in the 80s. A lot of our firm come from Newark, which is close to Lincoln, and the lads from each town hate one another. When we used to go there we'd stop on the way and pick the Newark lads up. As soon as we'd got into Lincoln we'd start scrapping with the locals. They've got about 50 football lads but that 50 are as game as fuck. For their numbers they are a top firm and I rate them highly. For numbers we'd swamp them but their 50 are top class. They don't really like Forest and they've got a main face at Man Utd in with their firm, who's meant to be a knock out specialist. They're fighters and they've always had a good England following. Go there if you want to have a night out, but if you cause bother the whole town will turn on you. It's fucking mental. I took two buses there on my 21st birthday and we ended up getting escorted out of town. The whole town turned on us as soon as we got there.

Orient

We went there in the F.A. Cup and had a fight with a group of black lads. There was about 30 of them hanging around outside the ground and we chased them up the road. We went in the Orient end just before the match got underway and no one said a word to us. We walked around the ground 40 handed and were so bored we went and stood with the rest of the Forest in the away end. I'd heard that you'd sometimes got a few West Ham going over there for the row. I'd been on the piss that day, big time, and when we chased the black lads I was knocked down in the road by a car. I didn't realise just how serious it was until the next morning when the drink wore off. I was in pain and was hobbling about. I went to the doctors and he gave me some painkillers and signed me off for the week.

Oxford United

They came to us twice in the 80s and got done both times. They attacked 'The Fountain', one of our pubs, and got chased everywhere. We were in the pub and half of our lot had left for the game when this Oxford lot walked straight in through the main door. We backed them off with stools and that and done a few of them outside the camera shop. The coppers came and nicked a few and I dived out the way and into a clothes shop. A lot of the Oxford lot got nicked for the fight and a few got put down. It made the headlines in our local paper. The 60 Oxford that came were well game, plus they'd come the year before, so you've got to give it to them, they're game. I know a few of their lads through the Mansfield lads and they've been up to Nottingham on nights out and they're decent lads. Credit where credit's due.

Bristol Rovers

They played at Forest many years ago in the League Cup and they bought a few lads and by all accounts done well. I hear they have a decent mob but then again I've never been down there.

Grimsby

They've been to Forest and came 60 handed and we had a right row with them on the bridge. We'd heard they were in town so about 30 of us split from our main mob and we found them about 1.30 p.m. and had a good toe-to-toe with them. They tried to throw one of me mates into the Trent from the bridge. We were outnumbered 2 to 1 but we still backed them off. We went up there the same season for a night game but it was called off. We only went up there because they'd come to us. We chased them all around Cleethorpes that day, but at least they turned up at Forest.

Chester

I don't think they've ever played at our place but I've been up there in the League Cup. We won something like 8-0, or something stupid. We was all over the town but didn't see anything. We didn't see them.

Shrewsbury

I know a few of the Shrewsbury lads through their friendship with a few of the Newcastle lads. I've heard they've got a decent little firm and they've got a big England following. They've made a bit of a name for themselves in the lower divisions.

Cambridge United

Some might say my 3rd team because it's my dad's town and team. A lot of their boys follow the London clubs but on their day they can still pull 60 to 70 game lads for certain games. They came to Forest in none other than, yes, you've guessed it, The League Cup. They turned up 40 handed and no one expected them to show. It had been pissing down with rain all day and I got a phone call to say they were here. We had no one out that night so I suppose they saw that as a bit of a result, a sort of a scalp of a big club. We went down there 30 handed, in a pre-season friendly and went in their end, and didn't see any of their lads, so it works both ways. I've still got a few family in Cambridge so over the years I've met some of their lads and they're good lads.

Cologne

I went out there when Newcastle played in a European game against the German side, Bayer Leverkusen. I didn't bother going to the game, which was being played in a stadium 10 minutes outside of Cologne, instead I stayed in the Irish bar and watched the game on T.V., and I noticed this lad keep looking over at me. He had Stone Island on and being a bit pissed I went over to him and said, "What the fuck are you looking at?" It turns out he was German and I'm thinking he's English and maybe even an English copper. After a couple of minutes, old Mr. Softy here buys him a drink and we carry on chatting. He thinks I'm a Newcastle fan but I explain I'm a Nottingham Forest Fan.

"I watch hooligan programmes on T.V. and I see Forest hooligans on T.V. I know Gary Clarke, I see him on T.V. He look good man." I stopped him dead in his tracks when I told him he was speaking to Gary Clarke. He looked at me blankly.

"I am Gary Clarke" I said, and showed him my passport, which I had on me. He couldn't believe it. His face changed from red to white and back through various shades before the colour came back into his cheeks. Since then we've become good friends and he's been over to England a few times to see me. I've been over for a few games in Germany and I went recently when they played Essen. They're a good bunch of lads that always make me feel more than welcome. They've got a good firm and they're all into the Stone Island and all the other English fashion labels.

Celtic

We played them in 83, in the UEFA cup 3rd round, and the first leg was at the City ground the game was on a Wednesday but the Celtic fans started arriving in Nottingham on the Monday morning. I was working in the market at the time, and all the fuckers were in the pub over there at five in the morning. On the day of the game, I think they took over every pub in the city centre except our pub, which was 'The Dog and Bear' they wouldn't come in their because all our lads were drinking in there. In the afternoon there was running battles in the main square and one of the Jocks was badly slashed across the neck and he ended up having something like 30 odd stitches a T.V. crew from Central were filming the clashes. At the ground, it was estimated that they had ten thousand fans at the game and it was going off all through the game it was none stop fighting, and I was loving it, them Jock piss heads were in every part of the ground and everywhere you looked it was going off. A couple of days after the game the coppers come and knocked at my house, to speak to me about this, Celtic lad that had been slashed. They showed me a photo of his injuries and went on to tell me that I'd been seen fighting on the T. V. footage, they went on to say that although they didn't think I was personally responsible for the attack, I might like to know that there was a reward out for information that could lead to the attackers arrest. I told them there and then to fuck off, and I never heard any more. The game finished in a 0-0 draw, and the 2nd leg saw us win 2-1. We only received less than two thousand tickets and although a Forest lad was treated for stab wounds the game passed off more peacefully then the home leg.

CHAPTER 14 ## Is That It?

FOREST HAVE gone into a rapid decline and we now find ourselves in the League One, which in old money is the old 3rd Division, and the season coming up 05/ 06 we will be playing the likes of Scunthorpe, Yeovil, and MK Dons. What's happened? We used to play Man Utd, Arsenal, Liverpool, and beat them and win the league and then we'd play in Europe and play teams like Barcelona, Ajax, Hamburg, Celtic, beat them and win the biggest prize of all but it seems them days are gone, and will they ever return? My current football banning order finishes in 2010 a week before the World Cup Finals start in South Africa so I'll see you all out there?

I've made a lots of good friends through following football and travelling over the years, and as my hooligan days are over I do keep in touch with a lot of lads from different parts of the world. I actually really don't dislike or hate anyone (even the sheep from up the road, just pity them). To me it was just a laugh and part of growing up (even though it took me thirty nine years).

You will never stop grown men fighting. I never fought anyone who didn't want it. I've never been a bully and never will be. I might have upset a few people along the way but that's life.

If football lads reading this book don't agree or think it's fiction then who gives a fuck? I've been as honest as I can be and it's how I saw it through my eyes. I never underestimate anyone big or small. Every football club has got a firm and anyone on their day can give someone a go. I always give credit where credit is due.

I love my football, always have done, always will do. Since I've been banned

I've started going to a few games abroad like Cologne or Real Madrid. Perhaps one day I'll go down to watch Forest again and no Old Bill will recognise me, which would be nice, and the crazy hooligan days would be something you read about in books. But we were there and we had the buzz, week in week out. No one will take that away.

It's been emotional,

Boatsy

P.S. I do hate someone, sex offenders and terrorists.

Me putting the finishing touches to this book.

Me and Kingy. We've become good pals since we met.

A few more from the German album...

Us, just 64 England lads overturned a German band on top of a bus.

Our lads squaring up to the Germans, police helicopter above, Turin 1990 .

Skeeny with American flag in the middle of Hamburg fans, prior to it kicking off.

Forest on tour, Munich 1979.

For further information on the Forest Executive Crew, speak to your football intelligence officer or enquire at your local police station, for an information pack.

Good Luck.